EM&LO'S **BUH BYE**

EM&LO'S BUH

THE ULTIMATE

DUMPING AND

GETTING DUM

BY EM&LO

ILLUSTRATIONS B

CHRONICLE BOOKS
SAN FRANCISCO

BYE:

GUIDE TO

PED

ARTHUR MOUNT

really do.

TEXT COPYRIGHT © 2007 BY
EMMA TAYLOR AND **LORELEI SHARKEY.**
ILLUSTRATIONS COPYRIGHT © 2007
BY **ARTHUR MOUNT.**
COVER PHOTOGRAPH COPYRIGHT © 2007
BY **DAVID JACOBS.**

LIBRARY OF CONGRESS CATALOGING-IN-
PUBLICATION DATA:
TAYLOR, EMMA (EMMA JANE)
BUH BYE : THE ULTIMATE GUIDE TO
DUMPING AND GETTING DUMPED / BY EM
& LO ; ILLUSTRATIONS BY ARTHUR MOUNT.
P. CM.

ISBN-13: 978-0-8118-5905-9
ISBN-10: 0-8118-5905-3

1.MAN-WOMAN RELATIONSHIPS.
2. REJECTION (PSYCHOLOGY) 3. SEPARATION
(PSYCHOLOGY). I. SHARKEY, LORELEI. II.
TITLE. III. TITLE: ULTIMATE GUIDE TO
DUMPING AND GETTING DUMPED.
HQ801.T285 2007
646.7'7—DC22
2007006091

MANUFACTURED IN CANADA

DESIGNED BY **AYAKO AKAZAWA**
EM&LO LOGO DESIGNED BY
AYAKO AKAZAWA AND **DAN SIPPLE**
TYPESETTING BY **JANIS REED**

DISTRIBUTED IN CANADA BY
RAINCOAST BOOKS
9050 SHAUGHNESSY STREET
VANCOUVER, BRITISH COLUMBIA V6P 6E5

10 9 8 7 6 5 4 3 2 1

CHRONICLE BOOKS LLC
680 SECOND STREET
SAN FRANCISCO, CALIFORNIA 94107

WWW.CHRONICLEBOOKS.COM

Acknowledgments

Thanks to all our friends and readers who shared their breakup stories, proving that heartbreak + time = comedy, at least half the time: Henry Abbott, Damian Barr, Tanya Bershadsky, Cathy Cavella, Gayle Dewes, Jennie Edwards, Robin Epstein, Saskia Fisher, Kiki Fries, Christian Haag, Kyja Helm, Nick Hughes, Amy Keyishian, Jamie Kirkpatrick, Melissa Kirsch, Tobin Levy, Erik Murnighan, Rachel Noel, Maite Quinn, Lorna Rutherford, Kelly Simms, Marielle Smith, Gwynne Watkins, Emily Wood, a bunch more who'd rather remain nameless, and, of course, those two dudes at the Jersey Shore (see **Dear John dot coms**). To the Chronicle gang, who continue to be too good to be true: Aya Akazawa, Leslie Davisson, Nancy Deane, Kate Prouty, and Jodi Warshaw. To Arthur Mount, for his genius illustrations. To David Jacobs, for somehow not capturing our utter embarrassment in his most excellent cover photo. To Ira Silverberg, for asking us to go steady. To all our exes, for the "material." To our sisters, Allyson, Becky, and Hannah, for buying the boxed wine in our times of need. And, finally, to Rob and Joey, for making the contents of this book feel like a distant memory.

Introduction

Unlike your best friend, this book doesn't take sides. Don't think of us as the bitchy, two-faced Heathers of the breakup world. We prefer to imagine ourselves as Switzerland, except with a sense of humor. Whichever side of the **chopping block** you're on, within these pages you'll find solace, instruction, and suggestions for inspirational T-shirt slogans.

If you just got dumped (or fear you're about to be), start on the very next page. **If you're about to dump someone** (or just did), start on page 10. These respective introductions will guide you toward the most relevant entries in this book. For a dose of sympathy, reverse the process. It's choose-your-own-adventure advice! Yay, breakups!

How to Get Over a Breakup
(in Ten Easy Steps)

So, you just got dumped. Come here, Lambchop, and let us give you a big hug. It's going to be all right. Really. Were you **downsized**? The victim of **frumping**? Did the bastard **fuck 'n' chuck** you? Did the bitch go **A.W.O.L.**? However bad it is, someone else has lived through worse before you—keep reading this book if you don't believe us—and they didn't lose their job or their marbles in the process. Sure, it might have been touch-and-go at first, but eventually they started bathing again. Some of them even got a promotion *and* fell in love with someone new. It's the cycle of life! Remember, bad breakups don't make you undateable, they just make you feel that way for a while—unless, of course, you lock yourself in your bathroom for the next year and refuse to answer the door for anyone except the Domino's guy. The following ten steps will keep you out of the john and in the human race. For more details on any given step, just read the full-length entries for the bolded terms following.

❶ **Numb the pain** for approximately seven days (two weeks max, in extreme circumstances). Everyone needs time to hit the wall, overeat, drink themselves silly, and generally self-medicate. Rent *Shirley Valentine* with a good friend. Get drunk on box wine. Lean on your friends, especially those who insist on referring to your ex as **Fuckface**. (If you suffer from the **hetero Harry handicap**, you might have to make do with listening to *Blood on the Tracks* on repeat, while eating Chinese straight out of the container, instead.) Make a **breakup mix tape**. Briefly consider **sexual reorientation**. Get drunk again.

❷ **Cut the cord**. As tempting as it may be to call your ex looking for **closure**, hoping to be **frexes**, or **ex-conning** them into **second-chance**

→

sex, this is *not* the time to concern yourself with **Fuckface**. In fact, as with smoking, going cold turkey is often best.

❸ **Think negatively** about your ex, especially if it helps you manage step two. Avoid looking back on your relationship with **rose-colored hindsight** or beating yourself up about what you did wrong. Learn from your mistakes (if you made any, which you probably didn't), and move on. And while you may hate your ex for dumping you, it's okay to claim to acquaintances, coworkers, and nosy family members that it was a **mutual decision**.

❹ **Git 'er done**. After you've broken down, it's time to rebuild yourself. You have it in you: start that political blog, dust off your bicycle, take that fiction writing class—after all, you're more than someone's other half. Haven't you always wanted to read ***Anna Karenina***? Never got around to painting your room because of all the time you wasted having sex? Do it now!

❺ **Give back to the community**. Nothing like volunteering at the local orphanage to put your heartache in perspective.

❻ Give yourself a **breakover**. If **revenge** is on your mind—and we know it is—get back at your ex by getting in the best shape of your life, getting the best haircut of your life, getting the best Botox . . .

❼ **Mark the occasion** of moving on with a **tattoo**, whether permanent or henna. Congratulations—you're more than two-thirds of the way through the breakup grief cycle already!

❽ Go shopping! It may sound a little Tri-Delt, but **retail therapy** can work by temporarily filling up that void inside you just long enough to get you through the next day. Go on; you deserve it. You can catch up on bills next month.

❾ Go on the **rebound**. Distract yourself with the joys of being single, so that you won't be tempted to claim any **W.M.D.s** or indulge in late-night **Googling** or other **e-spying** on your ex. Try **masturbation, online dating, flirting therapy, therapy fucking,** or **sympathy fucking**.

❿ **Think positively**. This is not the death of sex and love. This is the beginning. Say it again: This is the beginning! Now sing it: "**I will survive!**" Because you *will* survive. And you will **metabolize**. **Closure** will come. You might give in to **ex sex** and actually enjoy it, but if you do, make sure you're doing it for yourself and not because you're hoping for an **about-fuck**. Hey, maybe you should even go on a "date." (See **mourning period [for the dumpee]**. Though you might want to consider a **sorbet** first.) Remember, dating—whether online or off—is your chance to find better sex and truer love. **Fuckface** was just a stepping stone on your way to self-improvement, personal growth, and true happiness with the person you were truly meant to be with. Take comfort in the fact that, with every passing day, as the pain subsides, you're that much closer to your density. We mean, your destiny.

How to Break Up with Someone
(in Thirteen-and-a-Half Easy Steps)

So, you're about to dump someone. Should we give you a hug or a high five? We'll tell you right now to stop flipping through these here pages looking for our patented Painless Breakup Method—or at least permission to **pull a Shannen** by changing your phone number and having your doorman (or a **Dear John dot com**) break the news to your unloved one. Sorry, friend, it doesn't quite work like that.

Breaking up with someone means facing the music—the crying, wailing, Celine Dion-esque music that will make your ears bleed. It's going to feel shitty; it always does. But here's the good news: It won't feel nearly as shitty as being dumped. Of course, we're assuming, for the sake of these 13.5 steps, that this is a fairly traditional dump, i.e. one in which the dumpee deserves to be treated with a little tenderness. Besides, if you're breaking up with someone because they cheated on you in a three-way with your two best friends, then you're not *truly* a dumper anyway— you're just a victim of a **passive-aggressive breakup**. Turn back a few pages for How to Get Over a Breakup (page 7), then see **post-traumatic stress dis** or **mid-sesh smackdown** for how to get even.

But if you are indeed the dumper, there's more good news: You have a lot of control over how the whole thing goes down (at least, you do until you utter those four little words, "**We need to talk**"). That means there are ways you can approach the breakup to make the whole thing slightly less painful for your dumpee. And the less painful it is for them, the less painful it will be for you: diminished guilt, fewer tears, and the comforting knowledge that you could have been a total douche and gone **A.W.O.L.**, but instead you hung in there and bore witness to your dumpee's heartbreak, just like they needed you to. Here's how to do it like a champ and avoid excessive **collateral damage**.

❶ Before you start composing a perfectly succinct **Dear John**, make sure you're abiding by the **face-to-face imperative**. We don't care how micro the relationship was—even a one-night stand doesn't deserve a **white-out**, a **fuck 'n' chuck**, a **unilateral dump**, or a partner who goes **A.W.O.L.**

❷ Once you've put their heart through the blender, you can say good-bye to your "All Night Long" *Flashdance*-cut vintage concert sweatshirt (you were actually there! In 1984! Five rows from the stage!) that you left at the dumpee's apartment. So before you make a move, you might want to consider a preemptive **booty haul**. If your mission fails, consider it **lost property**. We think you'll get over it. It's not like you're about to get your ass dumped, after all.

❸ Don't be a **stealth dumper**. The kinder, gentler dumper knows to **pad the fall** first. By the way, **benching** someone for an entire season doesn't count as padding the fall, and neither does hanging tight until the end of spring semester to pull off a **passive breakup**, or acting like a total jerk in order to pull off a **passive-aggressive breakup**. And giving in to **rent control** is only padding your *own* fall.

❹ Choose an appropriate **chopping block**: don't do it over a **last supper**, know where **public displays of affliction** are and aren't appropriate, and don't be a coward and **pull a librarian**.

❺ Ready for **the Talk**? Don't beat around the bush and make them guess what you're trying to say: a **Band-Aid break** is the kindest approach. **Clichés** are kinder than **big fat lies**, which are kinder than the **cold hard truth**. Little **white lies** are a friend in need, but don't **overcompensate** with glowing praise, lest your dumper play **goalie** with your reasons for the breakup. And if you qualify for a **get-out-of-jail-free card** or a **doctor's note**, then use it!

6 If your dumpee is desperate, they may resort to **leg-clinging**, or even a scary **ultima-dump**. They may try to turn this into a **Teflon breakup** (one that won't stick). Be strong and stay on target—stay on target!—because a **noncommittal breakup** will only make things worse for your dumpee (and you) in the long run. Make sure you've alerted a **F.E.M.A.** to come pick up the pieces.

7 If there's **someone else**, have your answer to that question fully prepped—and don't stray from your script, no matter how your dumpee taunts you.

8 Don't say, "**Can we still be friends?**" if you're really talking about **endship**.

9 If your partner attempts to pull a **reverse dump**, just let it go. They need this more than you.

10 Like Kenny Rogers, know when to walk away: resist **one for the road** with all that you have in you. There'll be plenty of time later for **ex sex** or the ol' **booty bait 'n' switch**.

11 Now *stay* away for at least a few weeks, even if your dumpee turns into **Breakup Barbie** or Ken, even if you experience overwhelming **returner's remorse**, even if your ex calls begging for "**closure**." Your presence will only hinder their **healing process**—especially if you're feeling "confused" about your decision. After all, it's totally normal for you to miss your dumpee like crazy, even if the breakup was 100 percent the right decision. And you don't want to be doling out any false hope—because nothing turns the knife like a teary reunion followed two days later by a **groundhog dump**.

⑫ We know you've been ready to move on since, like, step two, but it's a nice gesture to abide by a respectable **mourning period (for the dumper)**, especially if you live in a small town or are cubicle-mates.

If you follow all these steps and still have a **bunny-boiler** on your hands, you might need to start preparing earlier next time around. Like, from the first date. **Emotional Imodium** and **disposable digits** were invented for folks like you.

½ But even if none of this works, at least reading this book cover-to-cover is the perfect excuse to postpone **the Talk** for a few more hours. That's gotta be worth the price of entry, right? Just don't leave the book on your partner's coffee table as a "hint."

A

about-fuck, an

Sex with your ex that's *so* good, the dumper does a 180 and gets back together with the dumpee; the post-orgasmic bliss-out "clears" their mind and helps them see that they were wrong to dump their Pumpkin and they really are meant to be together after all. Unfortunately, about-fucks are rarer than a good hair day for Donald Trump; if the brokenhearted could just admit this, there'd be a lot less pathetic **second-chance sex** happening (because no matter how much a dumpee's oral skills have improved, the dumper still won't want to date them). About-fucks, when they *do* happen, rarely stick for long, meaning that the poor ex in question gets dumped, then fucked, then fucked over. See also **groundhog dump**.

adultery

Sexual relations with **someone else**, i.e. *not* your committed partner, when these relations have not been explicitly or implicitly condoned by said partner. Also, one of the naughtier of the seven deadly sins (though less harmful to the waistline than gluttony). The term implies egregious lying and usually applies to a *married* adulterer, though the poor girlfriend or boyfriend being cheated on would probably beg to differ. If, or rather, *when* your committed partner finds out, brace yourself for a **post-traumatic stress dis**, **collateral damage**, and not getting into heaven.

alcoholism, temporary

One of the most common forms of **numbing the pain**. Not recommended if (a) actual alcoholism runs in your family, (b) you don't have a friend who's willing to act as designated dialer (see **drunken dialies**), (c) you've passed your thirty-fifth birthday, or (d) your friends are all twelve-steppers who won't help you finish the bottle. If, however, you're twenty-two and all your friends are out getting drunk off their asses every night anyway, there's nothing wrong with joining them and letting Mr. Daniels take the edge off your pain. See **numbing the pain** for specific rules on how long this period should last.

Anna Karenina

The perfect title to enjoy during your **git 'er done** period (though any great Russian novel will do). The sense of accomplishment will be massive, and you'll enjoy the brag value it provides when you start dating again. ("Oh yeah, I got my heart broken once, and I decided to read Tolstoy until I was ready to be social again.") Plus, when you read about (plot spoiler) a woman who dumps her husband, then commits suicide because she's afraid the man she left her husband for is going to dump her, you're really reminded that things could be *way* worse. However, please note that this title is specifically and exclusively recommended for the **git 'er done** period and is not to be attempted any sooner, lest the "it could be worse" effect is taken as a call to action.

A.W.O.L., going

When someone you're dating simply disappears into thin air—poof!—without so much as an explanation, even a short and lame one via e-mail or a lousy text message. In lieu of actually dumping you, they have simply gone absent without official

➜

A

leave. In junior high, this might be accomplished by telling someone, "I gotta go pee, wait here for me" during a slow dance and never coming back, leaving your date standing there in the middle of the dance floor for the remainder of Bryan Adams's "Everything I Do." If you're the dumper, you might think that hiding out somewhere (like, say, the bathroom) until your dumpee gets the message gets you off scot-free, but the guilt will get to you in the end—and so might your dumpee, if they're revengeful and resourceful enough. A.k.a. pulling a Cheney (you know . . . hiding out in an undisclosed location . . . no? too '01?). See also **disposable digits**, **face-to-face imperative**, **Fuckface**.

B

Band-Aid break

A quick and painful breakup—but certainly less painful than if the breakup occurs over a protracted period of time (see **noncommittal breakup**). If you're the dumper, once you've arrived at the **chopping block**, get to your point. Think of the breakup speech as a Band-Aid that needs to be ripped off fast, rather than tugged at torturously for hours. That said, the first words out of your mouth don't have to be "I'm dumping you." If you can make the breakup seem at least a *little* mutual, your now-ex will walk away with a modicum of pride, and you'll walk away sooner and with less guilt. Say "I can't give you X, Y, and Z," where "X, Y, and Z" are needs your partner has expressed to you. That way, they'll stew for a bit and then feel empowered because they're not settling for less than they deserve. It will make them feel involved in the process, which is key if you want to avoid a **reverse dump**.

bench, to

To put someone in relationship limbo without telling them. Let's say you have a sneaky feeling that you might want to break up with your partner soon, but you're not 100 percent sure, and in the meantime you don't want to screw things up just in case you're wrong. A grownup might confess these feelings of uncertainty, but that would lead to a big **Talk** (not to mention

an extended period of unreciprocated oral sex if you stay together after the Talk)—and all that yapping is precisely what you're trying to avoid right now. So you bench your partner and kind of hang out in relationship stasis, marking time until you've made up your mind whether to stay or go.

During this period, you may want to avoid any or all of the following: ❶ introducing your partner to any more friends or family members; ❷ committing to any double dates more than a week hence; ❸ leaving any large items of personal property at your partner's house (in extreme cases, you may actually start to retrieve particularly valuable/sentimental items of property from your partner's house on the sly, just in case— see **booty haul**); and ❹ trying out any new and daring sexual acts that might lead your partner to later accuse you thusly: "I can't believe you're dumping me right after I agreed to rim you!" By the way, if you actually break the rules of the relationship during a period of benching (e.g. by sleeping with someone else) rather than just withdrawing a little, then it is no longer officially referred to as benching; it is just plain cheating.

Someone who has been benched may not realize what has happened to them at first (that's the whole point, after all). And a brief period of benching is not a *terrible* idea—if you think you might be about to dump someone, it's best to postpone booking that nonrefundable vacation to Australia or avoid attending a family reunion together. (Nothing sends a mixed message like dumping someone the day after your sibling asks them to be a bridesmaid/groomsman.) This kind of behavior could be considered one aspect of what's known in the biz as **padding the fall**. However, if you let this benching period drag on for too long, it will become humiliatingly obvious to your partner (and, perhaps even worse, to all your mutual friends). At this point you will have crossed over into **passive-aggressive breakup** territory and will be experiencing what it feels like to be an utter jackhole. (A period of benching may also occur in the lead-up to a **passive breakup**.)

Finally, if you're the dumpee and feel like you just got **stealth dumped**, then you were probably benched for an entire season and didn't know it. A.k.a. breakup lite. Not to be confused with **unilateral dumping**.

between boyfriends/ girlfriends

A euphemism for one's pathetic state of singlehood, this phrase tries—and fails—to mask one's debilitating loneliness. As in, "I'm between boyfriends right now," suggesting that one is single by choice, man, *by choice*. The term is often overheard at family, high school, or college reunions, and used especially by the recently (or not-so-recently) dumped with friends/parents/colleagues who are overly inquisitive, condescending, or matchmaking-prone. For maximum believability, the phrase should be uttered with an air of exhaustion that implies one simply doesn't have the time/mental space/interest in commitment/clean underwear/focus to deal with a relationship right now. A.k.a. unemployed.

beyond my control

Classic dumping line uttered by the predatory Vicomte de Valmont to the naïve Madame de Tourvel, on the instructions of that control freak, the Marquise de Merteuil, in the 1782 French novel *Les Liaisons Dangereuses* by Choderlos de Laclos; in the 1985 Christopher Hampton play of the same name based on that novel; and, most famously, in the 1988 movie based on that play, *Dangerous Liaisons.* In the movie version (which starred John Malkovich, Michelle Pfeiffer, and Glenn Close in the respective roles), the scene is gut-wrenching to watch, and the setup horrifying and inhumane. However, the basic concept of not straying from a predetermined, generic explanation is not a bad one, especially if you're dumping someone with massive insecurity issues. Note the phrase *basic concept* here—the specific line "It's beyond my control" is annoyingly, insultingly evasive, and can only be pulled off by mildly sociopathic leading men and one particular friend of ours who used it on a guy who (a) had never seen the movie, (b) was kinda dumb, and (c) had cheated on her and therefore deserved to be taken advantage of regarding (a) and (b). See also **goalie, playing**, and **post-traumatic stress dis**.

B

THE MOST SOC
BREAKUP SCEI
DANGEROUS L

VICOMTE DE VALMONT (JOHN MALKOVICH): "I'm so bored, you see. It's beyond my control."

MADAME DE TOURVEL (MICHELLE PFEIFFER): "What do you mean?"

VALMONT: "Well, after all, it has been four months. So, what I said: it's beyond my control."

TOURVEL: "Do you mean you don't love me anymore?"

VALMONT: "My love had great difficulty outlasting your virtue. It's beyond my control."

TOURVEL: "Liar! Liar!"

VALMONT: "You are quite right, I am a liar. And it's like your fidelity, a fact of life. No more nor less irritating. Certainly beyond my control."

TOURVEL: "Stop it! Don't keep saying that!"

VALMONT: "Sorry. Beyond my control."

TOURVEL: "Do you want to kill me?"

IAISONS (1988)

VALMONT: "Listen. Listen to me. You have given me great pleasure. But I simply cannot bring myself to regret leaving you. It is the way of the world. Quite beyond my control."

See **beyond my control**.

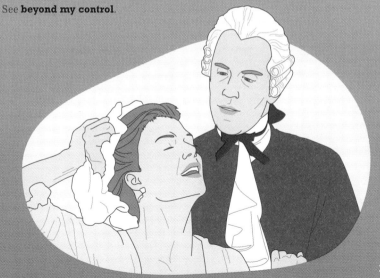

big fat lies

Obvious untruths lazily uttered by often well-meaning dumpers during many a breakup. While some **clichéd** breakups may *become* big fat lies down the road (especially when "I think we're just meant to be great friends" is followed by a decade of radio silence, a.k.a. **endship**, or an ex gets engaged three months after announcing "I'm not ready for a relationship right now"), a true big fat lie is more immediately discernible as bullshit than a **cliché**, which, no matter how tired, can still have some truth to it.

The top six big fat lyin' breakup lines of all time are:

❶ "I really need to focus on my career right now." *Riiiiight.* Even a recent leader of the free world had time for a wife and multiple mistresses—Bill even found time to buy Monica a freakin' souvenir sweatshirt, ferchrissakes! Nobody's career is so important or all-consuming that they couldn't take five for the right person. ❷ **Overcompensations**: "You're too good for me"/"You deserve better"/"You're really great, I'm just an idiot." Does anyone ever really believe these lines? We'd like to meet just *one* person who is so goddamn selfless that they'd give up a perfectly good relationship just so their ex could go on and find someone better-looking/better-paid/better-hung. Unless you're having a morning-after brunch with Mother Teresa, this line is strictly verboten. Besides, it's the sole responsibility of the **F.E.M.A.** crew to deliver this line of crap to the dumpee.

❸ "We met at the wrong time." Whenever we hear this line, we're reminded of that T-shirt slogan that goes, "How about never—is never good for you?"

❹ "I wish it could have worked out between us." Really? Well then why don't you rub the freakin' lamp and summon the Relationship Genie? Or better yet, get off your ass and *try* to make it work, you lazy fuck.

❺ "My parents don't approve of this relationship." Unless you're ten years old and on the right side of the tracks, or living in a country where they behead you

➔

B

for dating the wrong person, then this line will not hold up in our court of love. Sure, parents have been known to disapprove of their offspring's dating decisions in countries where beheading is frowned upon, but this is rarely the whole story. More like, "My parents would rather I dated within the Ivy League, and I would rather date someone with bigger boobs." ❻ "My friends are really important to me, and that's where I want to spend my time right now." In other words, "My friends are out getting drunk and laid every night, and I'd like to be doing the same thing."

While you might think telling the sorts of lies outlined above to someone you're dumping is mercifully innocuous, it's not. Try condescending and a tiny bit cruel. At least if you dish out a top-five **cliché**, then your dumpee will be able to commiserate with friends who will be all like, "Been there, heard that, felt your pain." But if you dish out a lie, then those friends will be all like, "Sure, sure, that makes sense—this is a really busy time of the year for pizza deliverers"

(while avoiding eye contact), and your ex will feel like shit.

On a final note, there are some smaller, less blatant lies that do not fall into this category and can sometimes be very welcome during a breakup—see **white lies** for examples and safety instructions for use. A.k.a. "This hurts me more than it hurts you." See also **lying under oath** and **someone else**.

Blood on the Tracks

Bob Dylan's 1975 opus that is widely regarded as the quintessential breakup album due to the nature of the material and the fact that Dylan's marriage of ten years fell apart while he was working on it. According to Dylan buffs, Dylan himself begs to differ, claiming that the album has more to do with Anton Chekhov's short stories than his own impending divorce. We might believe him if it weren't for songs like "If You See Her, Say Hello" and whispered lyrics like "I can change, I swear." Actually, given the spectrum of emotions covered, from the excoriating but kind of funny "Idiot Wind" ("You're an idiot babe, it's a wonder you still know how to breathe") to the heartbreaking and prophetic "You're Gonna Make Me Lonesome When You Go" (in which he gets grad-school sad and compares his relationship troubles to those of Rimbaud and Verlaine) to the reminiscing "Tangled Up In Blue" ("We always did feel the same, we just saw it from a different point of view"), *Blood on the Tracks* might be more accurately referred to as a *pre*-breakup album. Consider it Bob's pre-divorce "Dear Diary"—

a way to get a jump start on the whole **healing process** before the breakup was final (just don't tell any Dylan buffs). See also "Dumping Ditties" on page 186.

bondage

Something you should *never* engage in during **ex sex**, lest you end up with a reverse Mohawk, a missing eyebrow, or pictures of you on the Internet wearing nothing but adult diapers.

booty bait 'n' switch

The act of converting a broken-up relationship into a booty call, typically initiated by the dumper (if the dumpee initiates, they probably have ulterior motives—see **about-fuck**, **second-chance sex**, and **pageant sex**). If the following criteria are met, then the two parties probably *will* sleep together again: ❶ The sex was really good during the relationship. ❷ The breakup was really smooth (i.e. the dumper followed all the advice in this book and their partner didn't lose their shit/threaten suicide/take it out on the pet hamster). ❸ The two parties move in similar circles but aren't working on being **frexes**. ❹ Both parties stay single.

To avoid sliding back into relationship territory, the horny dumper should wait at least a month before booty-calling an ex, and make sure another month passes before calling them again. You can meet your dumpee for dinner or you can meet them for sex, but you can't do both—it's too much like a date. If you sleep over (though we wouldn't recommend it), keep the pillow talk light—chat about what you've been up to lately and don't invite your dumpee to hang out with you that weekend. No need to patronize them by saying, "You know this doesn't mean we're back together, right?" Simply hint at that with your actions: be hypervigilant about using condoms and dental dams (besides being plain common sense, it underscores the fact that it's casual sex); choose doggy-style over face-holding missionary; and keep the meaningful eye contact and lovey-dovey cuddling to a minimum. If you must refer to your past together, speak of it fondly but distantly, as if you were recalling your junior high prom date. Even better if you can joke about it, or, more specifically, joke about what a dork you were in the relationship. And if you're afraid you may accidentally blurt out

"Good god I love you" as you climax, then put a sock in it (literally).

booty haul

The act of retrieving your stuff (e.g. a favorite '80s concert T-shirt that you actually bought at a concert in the '80s, earning you serious ironic street cred) from your partner's apartment a few days before dumping them, because you know it will make you look petty to ask for it right after breaking their heart, but damn it, you fucking love that ratty old thing. See also **bench, to** and **lost property**.

bottom-feeders

People, usually men, who take advantage of the vulnerability of the recently dumped to get laid: you need a shoulder to cry on, they're there, then you're there with your pants off. Especially susceptible to the charms of bottom-feeders are those who've hit rock bottom, hence the name. Bottom-feeding, when "successful," is often followed by a **fuck 'n' chuck**. A.k.a. dumpster divers, rock-bottom-feeders.

break, taking a

Putting your relationship "temporarily" on hold in order to take a step back and get some perspective on things. In other words, to get the hell away from the person who's currently driving you crazy to see if you can do better . . . or at least get laid by someone else. Perhaps you've come to that point in the relationship where

→

it's time to shit or get off the pot, but you just can't decide: you're not ready to give up on it all together, but you're not sure you can make a bigger commitment . . . and so you'd like to get laid by someone else. Or perhaps you met your current partner in high school when you were a virgin and have spent the last ten years monogamous . . . and you just want to get laid by someone else.

Unfortunately, calling a time-out so you can have your cake and eat it too is like putting your elbow in your ear: damn near impossible. And so, nine times out of ten, taking a breather is a precursor to an "official" breakup. But people are greedy, delusional, hopeful bastards who will continue to insist on getting married a second time, playing the lottery, and taking mini-breaks.

So what if you find yourself with someone who's requested a break? Our gut instinct is that this is just a breakup that the person is too wimpy to commit to fully. But before you give in to our gut

instinct, you might want to seek advice from a higher power and ask yourself, *What would Sting do?* "If you love somebody, set them free," he said (though we don't think he invented the concept). The problem is knowing when and how often you're required to do this. Are you supposed to let someone "go free" for the rest of your relationship (and maybe your marriage), just to prove your love? Once a week? Just on special occasions? It seems to work for Goldie Hawn and Kurt Russell— she announced on *The View* that she never asks about his extracurricular activities. And they've been going strong for twenty-two years. (Unfortunately, she spoiled it by getting all Men-Are-from-Mars on the panel: "How would you like it, as women, to have testosterone running through your body every day, having to deal with this every day when they don't have control?" Poor things!)

If it's obvious that something needs to change in order to allay your partner's (and perhaps your own) fears about the future, and you're inclined to let your little bird fly like Sting (a pre-'90s, pre-tantric Sting, that is), then make sure you (a) explicitly outline the privileges of the break, and (b) give yourself those same privileges. If we learned nothing else from ten seasons of *Friends* (besides the facts that Emma is a popular baby name and leather pants are a bad idea), we learned that the terms of a break must be defined clearly by all parties before said break commences. Will you continue dating, but in an "open" relationship? Will you stay friends and keep each other in the loop on your dating activities? Will you date exclusively but go trawling for a three-way together every weekend? Will you break up but continue hooking up whenever you see each other? Will you agree to part ways and meet up again in exactly one year if you still want each other, à la *Before Sunrise*? Make sure these questions are answered satisfactorily. You'll still end up breaking up, but at least you'll be able to

have sex in the process too. See also **on a break**.

POST-BREAKUP   POST-BREAKOVER

breakover

A post-breakup makeover. When it comes to revenge (and if you're the dumpee, you know you want it), there are two approaches: the high road and the low road. A breakover is all high road—it's the kind of revenge that benefits you, rather than directly harming your ex, bodily or otherwise. Join a gym where you can literally work off all your anger and aggression in pursuit of a breakup body; the idea of **Fuckface** seeing you in the

→

best shape of your life will actually inspire you to work out longer and harder (listening to the *Flashdance* soundtrack also helps). Did your ex nag you for six months to quit smoking? Quit now. Take that, Fuckface! Get a new haircut, go shopping for a hot new wardrobe (see **retail therapy**), and make a shitload of money, either by winning the lottery or finally getting your own dance-studio business off the ground (see **git 'er done**, #1). Had the two of you always planned on trying erotic flogging for the first time, or experimenting with tantric sex, or visiting the neighborhood sex-toy shop, but never got around to it? Read *Jay Wiseman's Erotic Bondage Handbook*, rent *The Tantric Guide to Better Sex* from GoodVibes.com, splurge on a high-end sex toy from Babeland.com for you or your next partner, and put the sex you had with Fuckface to shame. Ha! A.k.a. eating their heart out.

break point

❶ In tennis, when the player *not* serving—i.e. the player supposedly at a disadvantage—needs only one more point to win the game. ❷ The moment during a breakup when the person doing the breaking up suddenly realizes that they are losing the upper hand—not to mention their cool—and that if they don't move quickly and decisively, they will be the victim of a career-defining **reverse dump**.

Breakup Barbie

A woman who appears unusually attractive after being harshly dumped: her eyes sparkle (because she's constantly on the verge of tears); she sheds that layer of winter insulation (because she hasn't eaten in two weeks); she's been going to the gym daily (because she wants to prove to her ex that he fucked up big time—a.k.a. breakup body); and her outfits

→

are fabulous (thank you, **retail therapy**). But be warned: This is not a woman who's undergone a healthy makeover, or rather, **breakover**. No, this is a woman on the verge of a nervous breakdown. So if you take a Breakup Barbie home from the bar, expect a horrifying scene of wailing and gnashing at 5:00 A.M. when her buzz wears off and she realizes that (a) he's never coming back, (b) you're a poor man's substitute for her ex, a.k.a. a **fucksimile**, and (c) she'll probably have to settle for someone like you. Don't take this personally, by the way—you could be George Clooney and she'd still call it settling. Okay, maybe not Clooney. But you could probably be a reasonably attractive B-list celeb and still suffer this indignity. Because while Breakup Barbie may be sparkly and pretty on the outside, her heart is as disfigured as Mattel Barbie's feet are from being forced to walk tippy-toe for all eternity. Steer clear, dude—go home and wank to your little sister's Barbie movie instead.

breakup mix tape

In the age of the iPod, this is an anachronistic yet quaint term for a playlist specially formulated to complement your post-breakup emotional state. Remember when you actually had to manually record songs, *while listening to them*, onto a cassette using a dual tape deck? While the process was long and labor-intensive, it gave one time to cry and contemplate; it was cathartic. Whatever your recording capabilities, you may find it therapeutic to create two playlists, where "Side A" is sad and weepy (Prince's "Nothing Compares 2 U" et al)

→

B

and "Side B" is angry, exuberant, and uplifting (Kelly Clarkson's "Since U Been Gone" et al). For more song suggestions, see "Dumping Ditties" on page 186. See also *Blood on the Tracks*.

bunny-boiler

A clingy, overbearing, vindictive, possessive, obsessive, unhinged, possibly suicidal (or, in rare cases, homicidal) ex. Named for Glenn Close's character who boils her ex-lover's daughter's pet rabbit in the 1987 classic drama *Fatal Attraction* (sample tagline: "The movie that will terrify men into being faithful"). A bunny-boiler refuses to take "It's over" for an answer. While the term is most often applied to women (hell hath no fury and all that), men can boil bunnies with the best of them (though they're more likely to be slapped with a restraining order before things get too out of hand). Bunny-boiler behavior includes, but is not limited to: ❶ Dialing your ex's number at 5:00 A.M. and then hanging up immediately, every night for a year, even though you know the ex has caller ID. ❷ Standing on the sidewalk outside your ex's window with a boombox raised above your head, blasting "Used to Love Her (But I Had to Kill Her)." ❸ Secretly befriending your ex's new partner and making them *your* new tennis partner. ❹ Faking a pregnancy. ❺ Threatening suicide (see **ultima-dump**). ❻ Stealing your ex's pet and holding it hostage. The difference between bunny-boiler behavior and garden-variety **revenge** or a **post-traumatic stress dis** is that bunny-boilers actually think they have a shot at winning back their ex—and therein lies the true crazy. A.k.a. number one fan (à la *Misery*), swimfan (à la *Swimfan*).

buyer's remorse

The regret felt after you've decided to pair up with someone, go steady, get married . . . i.e. "Oh god, what have I done?" Once your partner is off the market, they suddenly don't seem so great anymore. The newer models that keep popping up, like updated versions of Macs, are all shiny and cool, fast and easy. What you used to find sweet and endearing about your ex now drives you crazy: the way they eat with their mouth open (i.e. with gusto), the way they nag (encourage) you to get a better job, the way their grating (infectious) laugh makes your skin crawl (feel all safe and warm). It's a classic case of wanting what you can't have and not wanting what you *do* have. The grass looks greener on the other side, so you jump the fence, only to realize it was all an optical illusion. Then the **returner's remorse** sets in, making for a seemingly endless and annoying (at least to close friends) cycle of breakups and make-ups known as **eternal return**.

C

can we still be friends?

A popular breakup **cliché** used to wrap up **the Talk**, often signifying the beginning of an **endship**. While you may become **frexes**, each with a high **ex factor** that is sure to bum out any new partners you may acquire down the road, it's more likely that after a couple of weeks you will both be attracted to each other's **ex appeal**, end up having **ex sex**, and then be forced to endure another **groundhog dump**. So no, you can't still be friends.

celibacy

A period of temporary abstention as a form of breakup therapy. Celibacy can free you from all those anxieties associated with getting or having sex, so you can better focus on yourself (your career, your hobbies, your friends, your personal growth). You *could* spend all that free time looking for Mr. or Ms. Right— or you could just concentrate on yourself; after all, it's a law of nature that the minute you stop looking for a partner is the minute they show up. Plus, having sex (or not having sex) on your own terms can give you a sense of control (what the kids call "hand")—which is what most people are lacking after a bad breakup.

Post-breakup celibacy therapy is not for everyone, however. For example, if you recently emerged from a dull, sexless six-year relationship that left you feeling about as sought after as a chess nerd on prom night, then a couple of one-night stands or a friendly booty call might be just what the doctor ordered. But if you've just been dumped with the line "I'm not ready for a relationship right now" for the fourth time in as many months, then maybe some time on the wagon will help you regain your focus (not to mention your pride). Perhaps you feel that casual sex is getting in the way of you finding a fulfilling relationship. Don't think of it as a failure; think of it as a very elegant philosophy for celibacy! You don't necessarily have to swear off sex until you find your soul mate, but you could at least try staying celibate until you find your sense of self-worth. Basically, you should consider celibacy because it feels right to you and because you're being true to yourself—not because you're repressing some personal issue, insecurity, or trauma that stems from the breakup. Ideally celibacy happens around the time of the ninth step of the **healing process**—any sooner and you risk confusing it with isolation, loneliness, and nobody-will-ever-love-me-again-ness.

Given the rather hazy definition of "sex" these days, celibacy is what you make of it. Perhaps your brand of celibacy makes allowances for activities that can be accomplished fully clothed (yay, dry-humping!). Or perhaps you'll choose to stop

short of penetration. Or maybe you'll decide to completely shun the fairer sex (whichever sex you consider to be the fairer one), i.e. no hand-holding or make-out sessions either.

Ready to take the pledge? Start with a simple exercise in perspective. There *are* more important things in this world: world peace, a cure for cancer, TiVo. Sex, for all its wonderful pros, raises a hell of a lot of cons: risk of infection and disease, body image issues, limited contraception methods, unwanted pregnancies, lack of communication between partners, performance anxiety, sexual incompatibility, unrealistic expectations, religious and/or societal guilt, impolite emissions, etc. With a list like that, why don't more people give celibacy a chance?

Besides the little congenital detail that we were made to fuck in order to propagate our species (that, and it just feels good), there's our sex-soaked culture to blame. Everyone from car companies to instant rice makers use sex to sell their

➜

products; magazines highlight the same recycled article about it on each month's cover; most TV shows and movies feature it as a subplot at the very least; cottage industries (like ours) have been built upon it; and e-mail spam forces it down your throat every day. With this kind of inundation—what is in effect a sort of peer pressure—it's no wonder Americans spend so much time, effort, and money to ensure they keep having sex regularly, at least as often as the Joneses. But with more sex comes more heartbreak—when it's all about quantity, the quality suffers.

To just say no to all this takes some serious guts. It's definitely the path less traveled, and you may feel like the odd man or woman out. But you're actually in good company: Ovid, St. Catherine, Joan of Arc, Leonardo da Vinci, Elizabeth I, Gandhi, and Josh Hartnett in *40 Days and 40 Nights* are just a handful of the many hip, non-creepy people who have taken vows of celibacy. Though they each had a different motivation for banishing the booty, for all of them it would seem to have served its purpose. None of them had blind faith in celibacy for its own sake; rather, they chose it because of how it would somehow advance their own personal goals (be they victory for France or a career in Hollywood).

Now remember, just because you temporarily stop having sex doesn't mean you stop being sexual. And denying yourself shouldn't be part of the post-breakup philosophy. It's not like you're conserving your mojo for some big fight. If your ultimate goal is to improve your own sex and love life, then there's plenty you can be doing on your own to do just that. Take this opportunity to spend some quality time with yourself. Ladies, get to know your body and how it works and what it likes, teaching and training yourself to climax via different methods. Gentlemen, you know the drill. (See **masturbation**.)

Before you get too excited (or would that be unexcited?), you should know that a self-imposed bout of post-breakup celibacy can have its own down-sides. Like virgins who are postponing sex until they find the perfect partner with whom to "share their gift," you run the risk of overbilling the big event. With every passing year that an adult virgin waits to have sex, the stakes are raised, and thus the more perfect that perfect partner needs to be. In fact, no one can be that perfect, and suddenly our virgin is forty and has never been kissed. While we applaud the decision to take sex a little more seri-ously, we would hate to see anyone build it up to be this monolithic, mythical thing. Even if you do eventually find someone to connect with on fundamental levels, you won't be able to connect with them on *all* levels. Also, knighting them as The Worthy One puts a lot of pressure on them and on the relationship to meet your hyper-high expectations, With any relationship, there are bound to be at least a few dis-appointments. Waiting to have sex until you feel totally com-fortable may help decrease the

potential disappointments, but it will never get rid of them completely. And don't forget that sex *is* just another "funda-mental level" you need to con-nect on. Sometimes it's better to find out if you're sexually compatible before investing too much (time, emotional energy, homemade greeting cards) in a relationship that you hope will be sexually satisfying in the long run.

On a final note, this book does not endorse the use of words such as "cult," "born-again," or "virgin" in describ-ing your sex-free lifestyle. Remember, celibacy might be a long and scary ride, but you can get off (in more ways than one) any time you like.

Chicken Little syndrome

The inability to believe that your totally hot/smart/funny/rich partner is just that into you, and the resultant obsessive need to snoop on said partner. You remember Chicken Little, right? She was so convinced that the sky was falling that she failed to notice what a beautiful, cloud-free day it was—no sky-chunks in sight! And she was such a glass-half-empty bird that she couldn't possibly believe that what she felt was simply a harmless acorn conking her on the head. She put more stock in the neurotic assumptions inside her tiny chicken brain than she did in what was actually going on around her.

Sufferers of Chicken Little syndrome drive themselves—and, ultimately, their partners—crazy with the fear that their relationship is about to crash and burn. Instead of enjoying all the great sex, belly laughs, and fancy dinners, instead of congratulating themselves on finally finding a partner who is worthy of all their "assets," they lie in bed at night counting the ways their partner must be cheating on them. Every time their partner doesn't pick up their work phone, they assume they're being orally pleasured under their desk; every time a bartender says hello, they assume it's a former ex/current booty call; every time their partner suggests a walk on a secluded beach, they assume **the Talk** is coming. Chicken Littles are exhausting to date, and thus the syndrome can be, unfortunately, rather self-fulfilling.

If you're suffering from the syndrome, what you need is a good ol' Oprah-style attitude adjustment. All those "friends" you're introduced to, those exes, those outgoing calls on their phone you don't recognize, those charges on their credit card statement you can't place—they're just acorns. Some people deal with acorns better than others—they figure, hey, thank god it's not bird

→

poop. But others either have a bad case of paranoia (for which you might want to seek professional therapeutic/psychiatric help) or are just too darn negative (in which case you need to follow our advice to the letter, read some self-help books, and do some damn yoga).

Whichever the case, if you are a Chicken Little you definitely need to go cold turkey (or would that be cold chicken?) on all the snooping. No more checking their cell phone. No more questions about their exes, **frexes**, or so-called "friends." Don't even think about trying to figure out their e-mail password. And you may as well toss out that amateur fingerprinting kit you ordered off the Internet, too.

Sure, if you happen to have found yourself a lying, cheating asshole of a partner, then all your detective work *might* uncover their dirty deeds sooner than you'd find them out in the natural course of things (see **worst-case scenario breakup**). But if that's your only means of telling whether you're dating a lying, cheating asshole, then we think you need to work on your intuition (or your taste in dating partners). Most likely, though, your snooping around will get *you* caught out—and after someone's caught you snooping once, it'll take them a long time to trust you again. More likely than not, they'll just dump you then and there.

In the meantime, the obsessing is just kind of a bummer. When you're feeling insecure, you can read anything into anything, so you've got to protect yourself from the tailspin that it might launch you into. The next time you're tempted to pry, force yourself to crack open your own journal instead, and write down the most recent nice thing your extremely good-looking partner has done for you. Or write down the last compliment they paid you. If you're not the journal type (we know, it's kind of an after-school-special suggestion), then try this instead: make a list of all the activities that make you feel good about yourself—perhaps it's going for a run, hosting a ladies'/boys' night, calling your mom, visiting the old folks' home, renting **Shirley Valentine**, renting porn, putting money in someone else's expired parking meter. Force yourself to do one thing on this list every time you're tempted to pry.

Don't beat yourself up about the occasional slip or your past snooping, though—we've all been there. Rather, think of every time you choose *not* to snoop as proof that there's a secure, happy person inside you just dying to get out.

You see what we're working on here? S-E-L-F E-S-T-E-E-M. There's no overnight fix for it, unfortunately, but we *can* tell you that the fastest way to feel like shit about yourself is to engage in behavior you know is wrong just because of a few harmless acorns. There's a reason your partner picked you, and as long as you're not the offspring of some celebrity they've been obsessing over since sixth grade, we're pretty sure they actually like you for

you. They like you, they really like you!

Of course, mistrusting someone for no good reason and then snooping on them are both perfectly legitimate reasons for them *not* to like you. How ironic if they ultimately leave, not because they've found someone else, but because you're a snoop, or because you never trust them (even though they've given you no reason not to), or because you're a great big ball of stress. That would be a tragedy of Greek proportions.

Yeah, maybe someday your partner won't like you quite as much, for some other random reason. But maybe some day *you* won't like *them* quite as much. Or maybe you'll get hit by a bus, or maybe they'll grow a mullet—that's life. And these things are all beyond your control, so there's no use in worrying about them. Relationships change, people change; sometimes people make mistakes, sometimes they don't. The only thing obsessing about the "what ifs" is guaranteed to do is drive you nuts. You can either enjoy the ride and be bummed when it ends, or you can have a terrible time on the ride, worrying about it ending, and then *still* be bummed when it ends.

But maybe it'll never end. Maybe you'll get married to Mr./Ms. Too-Good-To-Be-True and have 2.4 devastatingly good-looking kids who'll play with your hypoallergenic golden doodle in your white picket-fenced yard, and you'll all live happily ever after. It's not something we'd bet money on, but it's more likely than the sky falling.

chopping block, the

The scene of the dump. Like real estate, clean breakups are all about location, location, location.

If it's a fairly new or light-hearted relationship, then pick a place where you and your dumpee won't be interrupted. It shouldn't be too public, but it shouldn't be too intimate, either—not your office cafeteria (that says you're squeezing them in between meetings), but not in bed after you've just screwed (that says you're a heartless monster—see **fuck 'n' chuck**). You're going for neutral territory. A park bench will do, as long as that's not where you first told your partner "I think I could fall in love with you." If it's cold out or you need a drink to get your nerve up, a bar is fine as long as it has a quiet corner and it's not their local joint (they'll have to find a new spot to drown their sorrows in) or the site of your first date (you'll unnecessarily taint what *could*

→

C

remain a beautiful memory for them). You'll want to set a time limit: do it before it gets dark out, lest you lose track of time and beers and end up losing your nerve. Whatever you do, don't take them to dinner, i.e. the **last supper.**

If you've been dating seriously and/or your ex-to-be tends to react "strongly"—i.e. they may throw up upon receiving the bad news—then do it somewhere private (and don't wear anything white). You should be willing to travel to their neck of the woods; don't make them take a ten-dollar cab ride to your house just so you can kick them out when they get there. Also, you don't want them to suffer the further indignity of having to ride the subway home with snot and tears dripping all down their face while hordes of travelers pretend not to notice their pathetic sobs. If their neighborhood is all out of non-descript coffee houses, then suggest a gentle stroll. If it's monsoon season, then doing it at their place may be the most convenient: it's private, you can pick up your favorite T-shirt and toiletries, and they don't have to travel far to crash face-down on their bed. However, the bad energy of the scene has the potential to disrupt the feng shui of their apartment for months to come. Are you sure you really have to do this? See also **public displays of affliction**.

C

clichés

While every breakup is a cliché to some extent (did you really think you were the first person in the history of relationships to be dumped for a RealDoll?), there are certain phrases a dumper can use that have been uttered so many times in so many breakups that they now convey about as much emotion as noting, "Terrible weather we're having for this time of year, eh?" The following top five clichéd dumping lines are typically preceded by the all-time cliché **"We need to talk"**: ❶ "I love you, but I'm not in love with you." Literal translation: "I no longer find you attractive—if I ever did—and the thought of sleeping with you now repulses me. Please don't cry." ❷ **"It's not you, it's me**." Literal translation: "You want to be in this relationship and I don't." ❸ "I'm not ready for a relationship right now." Literal translation: "I'm not ready for a relationship with *you*." (See **fortune cookie rule**.) ❹ "You want more than I'm prepared to give." Literal translation: "You want more than I'm prepared to give to *you*." (Ditto.) ❺ "I think we're just meant to be great friends." Literal translation: "I'd like to keep sleeping with you if that's okay with you." (See **booty bait 'n' switch**.)

While no one ever wants to be handed one of these clichés word-for-word (it's like being dumped by a Hallmark card), the basic concept—to avoid hurtful specifics and maybe even make the dumpee feel good about themselves—is benevolent. So if you're about to dump someone for one of the above five reasons, do them a favor and put the phrase in your own words—it'll make them feel like you stewed over this decision for more than five minutes. Sure, they'll probably beg you for specifics, but don't give in! In the long run, this breakup will be a whole lot smoother if you can keep it vague. A particularly astute dumpee may ask, somewhat sarcastically, "So basically what you're saying is, it's not me, it's you?" Or worse, "So basically, what you're saying is, the thought of sleeping with me now repulses you?" Be warned: They're just trying to trap you into giving up more details. Don't do it! Because while your ex will whine for a few days to their friends about

➔

how "lame" it was to be dumped with a top-five cliché, it's nothing compared to how one tiny, specific, ugly detail will rattle around in their head for the next decade—see **cold hard truth** for more on this kind of behavior and why you should avoid it. A.k.a. killing them softly, yada yada dump, "You're fired!" See also **big fat lies** and **doctor's note**.

closure

❶ A calm, rational talk several days, weeks, or even months after the more emotional **Talk** (during which one of you probably cried hysterically, shouted profanities, hit something, and/or almost threw up). After the original Talk, the dumpee usually stays up all night trying to figure out what went wrong, going over every single thing the dumper said, and replaying the last three months in their mind on slo-mo, looking for any clues that should have tipped them off to the impending doom. This will go on for

several days, weeks, or even months—and then they'll *really* want to talk about it. That's when they'll ring up the dumper looking for "closure," which is really just a fancy term for the dumpee asking more questions that they really don't want answered. If the dumper has no interest in remaining friends, then it's okay for them to say no to this line of questioning— what is known as **foreclosure**. Because the more the dumper humors the dumpee, the more likely the dumper is to accidentally blurt out the **cold hard truth**. And that's when the dumpee will *really* throw up. ❷ **Ex sex**. ❸ **Revenge**. See **post-traumatic stress dis**.

cold hard truth

A particularly damaging ingredient of some breakups, utilized by dumpers who feel that it's "only right" to be "completely honest" in their little breakup speech, as if they've just been lassoed by Wonder Woman. These breakups may leave dumpees reeling for years, thanks to the specific "facts" that the dumper throws in. It can make a person long for the good old days of **clichés** (or hell, even **big fat lies**). The brutally honest approach is the opposite of a clichéd dump: it is *incredibly* personalized. Your very own breakup! If this sounds like a good thing, here are some particularly egregious examples we've collected over the years from friends, acquaintances, readers, drunks at the end of the bar, and personal experience: ❶ "I just don't find you all that attractive." ❷ "Do you realize how much weight you've gained since we met?" ❸ "I just never expected you to age so badly. Does your dad wear a toupée or something?" ❹ "I need to break up with you so I can bang the girl you always think I have a crush on." ❺ "You're not the one I picture getting married to or being buried alongside." ❻ "Do you eat a lot of garlic? Your breath is just kind of overwhelming." ❼ "Do you have a lazy eye? You always seem to be looking over my shoulder when we're about to kiss." ❽ "I just can't date a premature ejaculator." ❾ "I guess I just always imagined myself ending up with someone who cared about their career." ❿ "You remind me too much of my mom."

In extreme cases, your Honest Abe may break out an entire shopping list of your faults, all in the name of "being up-front." And in the mother of all scenarios, your dumper may explain why their new hot coworker exhibits none of these faults.

You might think that you'd have to be raised by wolves to dump a partner with such little tact. The problem is, the most well-intentioned breaker-upper can sometimes get sucked into this by a masochistic dumpee who refuses to settle for anything less than the cold, hard, insulting, unabridged truth. Here's the thing: Dumpees can't handle the truth! And they rarely actually want it, no matter what they say. If you're the dumper, you're already putting a knife in their heart—don't turn it with

→

specifics. So when they ask you why, say that you're not ready for anything serious, you think you're meant to be friends . . . whichever one of the **clichés** is closest to the truth (feel free to improvise—ours is by no means an exhaustive list).

When your dumpee asks, "Is it because I didn't do X, Y, and Z?" or "Why am I not good enough for you?" or "What do I have to fix to get you to stay?" the answer is always, "**It's not you, it's me**"—except, of course, you never, ever use that exact phrase! Say, "You're smart and funny and hot" or "Our time together has been really fun"— and then remind them that you're just too different to work together long-term. In other words, you're offering up something that's definite and irrefutable, yet still leaves the dumpee with the sense that they won't die alone, that *someone* out there will want them. These little compliments will give your dumpee something to cling to—they're like life vests in the miserable days and weeks after a breakup.

collateral damage

Harm or injury (emotional or physical) resulting from a bad breakup: vases thrown during temper tantrums, walls punched (i.e. hands broken), vacation pictures cut up or burned, child visitation rights limited, favorite items forever left behind (because you can't return to the scene of the breakup—see **lost property**), jobs lost due to excessive **numbing of pain**, and friends lost because they're forced to take sides (not *your* side).

THE MOST ENE
BREAKUP SCE
SAY ANYTHIN

DIANE COURT (IONE SKYE): "I think we should stop going out on dates."

LLOYD DOBLER (JOHN CUSACK): "Oh. I feel like a dick. You must think I'm a dick."

DIANE: "No, I don't. I don't."

LLOYD: "Yeah, you do."

DIANE: "Lloyd, we shared the most intimate thing two people can share."

LLOYD: "Yeah, you shared it with a dick."

[Quickly followed by the world-famous "In Your Eyes" on Uplifted Boombox Post-Breakup Scene.]

EARING MOVIE
E OF ALL TIME:

(1989)

command-Z

As in, "Undo! Undo!" All the stuff that you say in the heat of the breakup moment and immediately wish you could take back, from the angry ("You never ever ever made me come"—see **match point**) to the pathetic ("I'll wait for you, I'll always be here in case you change your mind"—see **leg-clinger**) to the slightly psychotic ("If you leave, I'll skin my cat"—see **ultima-dump**). See also **ctrl-ex**. A.k.a. ctrl-Z (for PC types).

common-law monogamy

Exclusivity that is established not by a "let's go steady" talk, but rather by the amount of time spent together and the number of family members introduced. While we are usually the queens of the no-assumption rule—i.e. don't assume monogamy until you've shaken on it—there are some circumstances where the rule is no longer in effect. Say you've been dating for a year, the two sets of parents have met, and you've suffered through a **pet dump** to relieve your partner of their Fluffy-induced allergies . . . well, at this point, actions say more than words (it ain't just an excellent Extreme song, it's the truth). When some cheaters are confronted and about to be dumped, they may try to invoke the "we never had the exclusivity talk" loophole. At this point, you should feel free to slap that phony with a common-law monogamy lawsuit—in other words, you will carefully explain that the two of you are, in fact, an item, and that if your partner wishes to sleep with other people, they will first have to actually break up with you.

crappy departing gifts

Swag a dumper gives to the dumpee as a peace offering or a token of their appreciation during a breakup: ratty T-shirts tainted with their B.O., their framed graduation photo, a favorite Bic (à la *Say Anything*: "I gave her my heart, she gave me a pen").

crappy holidays

Christmas, New Year's, and Valentine's Day—the three days out of the year when you *really* wish you weren't broken up.

You're not alone. Well, sure, you're alone in the sense that you don't have a cutie to go ice-skating with while clad in matching striped scarves from the Gap. But you're not *alone* alone. Despite the onslaught of trailers for overly sentimental flicks featuring inspirational sports teams/family reunions/ elf costumes, all those extra DeBeers commercials (that actually make us pine for the Coors twins), and the music about love and joy that's piped into every pharmacy—despite all that, love is not, actually, all around. There's war and infidelity and existential crises and depression and people in those pharmacies fighting and pushing to get to the front of the line with their gift wrap, emergency box of tampons, and prescription meds. It only feels like love's all around because single people don't spend as much money on holiday gifts and activities, so as far as Madison Avenue is concerned, you're persona non grata. You might as well be an elf. So you and the other (newly) single people start hibernating—drinking Coors in dive bars, most likely— which makes you feel even more alone. During this season, you might find yourself linger- ing in the self-help aisle at your local bookshop, fingering titles like *If I'm So Wonderful, Why Am I Still Single?* and *Healing Your Aloneness: Finding Love and Wholeness Through Your Inner Child.* (We wish we could say we made those titles up.) This extended season is a romance pressure cooker guaranteed to make you feel like the kind of loser who might actually *buy* one of these books.

But maybe all your inner child needs is to pig out on some chocolate wrapped in red foil and a few Morningstar Farms Mini Corn Dogs. The holidays never used to suck when you were a kid, even if Jeanie from the third grade didn't get you a Christmas card. And it would never have occurred to you to pine for Jeanie on Christmas morning, because you were too busy ripping open your presents and watching your grandmother get soused. Give thanks this year that your to-do list for the season is as uncomplicated as when you were six—except this time around, you're allowed to get drunk, too!

And there are other blessings to be counted. You get to enjoy a year off from celebrating the holidays with someone else's annoying and/or dysfunctional family—no pretending to like their mom's Jell-O mold or fake-laughing at their dad's bad jokes. You don't have to worry that your partner will embarrass you in front of your family by burping, swearing, or talking about your oral sex acumen. And think of all the money you're saving on presents! You don't have to fret over whether your partner will break the ten-dollar limit you agreed on, thereby making you look like a cheap bastard. You can get drunk at the office holiday party and gossip with all your coworkers without having to make your partner feel "included," and then you can make out with someone highly inappropriate and pretend to be embarrassed about it for the rest of the year. Best of all, you can wear your comfy pants with the elastic waistband so you can properly indulge—after all, there's no annoying girlfriend or boyfriend around to complain that they make you look like George Costanza.

Other steps you can take to survive this trifecta from hell include: doing your shopping early to avoid the worst of the commercial Cheez Whiz; getting together with your single friends and talking shit about your ex *and* all your annoying lovey-dovey coupled friends; volunteering at a soup kitchen to put your own crappy holidays in perspective. But whatever you do, don't **impulse buy** a boyfriend or girlfriend just because everyone tells you it sucks to be alone at the holidays. Remember those "a puppy is for life, not just for Christmas" ads? Don't confuse warm, fuzzy yuletide feelings with the desire to be in a relationship—it's not true love, it's just the eggnog. And the hangover's a bitch. A.k.a. the unholy trinity of holidays.

ctrl-ex

Breaking up with your PC because it's difficult, unreliable, and boring, and beginning a beautiful long-term relationship with a Mac, because it's laid-back, good-looking, and fun to be with. See also **command-Z**.

cutting the cord

Forced amnesia as an essential tool in getting over a recent breakup, and step two in the **healing process**. This is *not* the time to concern yourself with being friends and making nice with **Fuckface**. In fact, we think cold turkey is in order at this point. Cut off as much contact as possible (please don't tell us you dated your coworker or roommate). Sure, you're inevitably going to obsess over them for some time to come, with **rose-colored hindsight** ("Who will pick my bacne now?"), but this is best

C

done in your own company, not theirs. Specific steps you should take at this point include: removing the ex from your speed dial, deleting all the cute e-mails they sent you, burning all their photos, etc. (This may or may not involve some kind of ritualistic ceremony with candles, incense, and chanting.) A.k.a. **spring cleaning**.

deal-breaker

Something you discover about your partner that leaves you with no other choice but to immediately and automatically dump them (or at least not call them for a second date or a second fuck). Common deal-breakers include, but are not limited to: incurable halitosis; still lives with Mother; has a criminal record; smokes; smokes crack; is a first cousin; once dated your best friend/sibling/parent; votes for the American Idol but not for local politicians; listens to Celine Dion; uses the word "gay" to mean "lame" in a junior-high way; gets upset if you use the word "gay" to mean "lame" in a junior-high way; refuses to use a condom or get tested; porno addiction; **adultery**; adultery with your best friend/sibling/parent; adultery with a goat. They're also known as standards, and they're neither watertight

→

C

nor beerproof. You might also find that, with age, your long list of deal-breakers gets smaller: after two decades of disappointing dating, for example, you might discover that "don't be a cokehead" and "don't hit me" are all the criteria you really need.

Dear John

A letter, e-mail, passed note in class, text message, Post-it note, skywriting display, or singing telegram sent to inform the receiver that the sender would like to discontinue the relationship, thank you very much.

Traditionally, a Dear John is carefully and thoughtfully handwritten on a nice piece of stationery and then strategically placed where the recipient will see it when they arrive home (they will inevitably be carrying a $10 bouquet of just-because flowers for their loved one at the time). But no amount of good penmanship can make up for the fact that Dear Johns are basically selfish, cowardly

acts that rudely reject the **face-to-face imperative**. Leaving a note forces the dumpee to take the initiative if they want to respond (and they have a right to respond). Instead of just conveniently hitting "reply" on an e-mail (the best form of Dear John available) or throwing a drink in their dumper's face, they're forced to call up their dumper or track them down for the closure they deserve— an *added* humiliation to the breakup in the first place. One dump like this can give off aftershocks that the dumpee will be reeling from for years. Take one friend of ours who flew across the country for her cousin's funeral, and returned to the apartment she shared with her boyfriend to discover that all his stuff had been removed, and in its place was a breakup letter. It's stories like this that can destroy one's faith in humanity.

But even worse than the Dear John letter is the Dear John *note,* a.k.a. the found breakup. Vehicles include Post-it notes (cf. the *Sex and the City* episode "The Post-it Always

D

Sticks Twice," wherein Berger dumps Carrie with a sticky), recipe cards, envelope backs, lightly soiled napkins, and telephone message pads. Just in case we need to spell it out, here are just a few of the reasons why coldly giving *note*-ice like this sucks big time: ❶ It sends the message that you, the dumper, consider the breakup to be on a par with shopping lists and adhesive reminders to give the dog his meds. ❷ It feels rushed and spontaneous, like it was something you just thought of as you were walking out the door. ❸ It's got that creepy "I was right here but couldn't actually face you, so I left through the bathroom window right before you showed up" vibe. ❹ Leaving notes for each other is a lighthearted but intimate act that is one of the cutesy privileges of cohabiting or owning a copy of each other's keys. Leaving a breakup note seriously abuses this privilege. Besides, if you know them well enough to own a set of keys to their place, what the hell are you doing leaving a note?! (Again, see **face-to-face imperative**.)

The *only* exception to our ban on notes is if you're creeping out of someone's apartment after a one-night stand, and you want to leave a "thanks for the butt sex!" note (with or without your phone number). But even then, this kind of note is acceptable only if the previous night's encounter was explicitly and mutually agreed upon as a one-night-only special. If, on the other hand, you lured the person to bed with promises of walks in the rain and weekend visits to your place in the country, then the usual rules—as outlined in the **face-to-face imperative** entry—apply. See also **fuck 'n' chuck** and **public displays of affliction** (def. #2).

Dear John,

I'm Audi 5000

Thanks for the memories,
Your now-ex

Dear John dot coms

Web sites that do your dirty work for you, including the actual DearJohn.com site that will generate and send a poorly punctuated, terribly impolite, Mad Libs–style breakup e-mail on your behalf. Breakupbitch.com and Breakupbutler.com are sibling sites (from the creators of the **Rejection Hotline**) that deliver audio breakup messages to your dumpee's phone for twenty cents a pop, tailored to fit the relationship you're walking out on (from friends-with-benefits to fiancés . . . though anyone who dares use this service for the latter should be stranded on a desert island with Carrot Top for at least a decade). Prospective dumpers who require more of a "personal" touch can hire someone to actually make the call (*seriously* creepy).

Unfortunately—actually, make that *fortunately*—this line of business does not appear to be a particularly lucrative one, as the Internet is littered with now-defunct breakup services like this (including the incongruously cheery DumpMonkey.com, which, for the bargain price of $24.95, would break up with your partner over the phone *and* send them a commemorative monkey). Which makes us think (okay, *hope*) that most of the traffic on sites like Breakupbitch is due to surfers who like to forward their friends "funny shit" when they're supposed to be working for the Man. In other words, this kind of thing is usually at its best in a bar at 2:00 A.M. when your totally stoned buddy is like, "You know what we should totally do, dude? We should build a breakup site so we don't have to break up with any more chicks!" You totally high-five each other, go back to your apartment to register EZbreakup.com, and then spend the rest of the summer at the Jersey Shore telling everyone about your totally awesome business idea. (Seriously: if you hung out at a bar in the Point Pleasant area anytime during the summer of '06, you probably heard about this one.)

On a final note, sites like Ijustthoughtyoushouldknow.com will deliver anonymous personal hygiene tips ("You've got bad breath"; "You stink," etc.) if you *don't* want to end the relationship but are convinced that actually delivering the much-needed message yourself would lead to a breakup. See also **disposable digits**, **face-to-face imperative**, **wakaresase**.

deep-six

To break up with someone in such an intense and definitive manner that the dumpee feels like he or she has been thrown overboard and is bobbing in a rough sea of despair without a life preserver. "She deep-sixed me. I came home to find all her stuff gone except for a **Dear John** letter on a fucking Post-it note, no less."

desperate measures

The crazy shit you do to win an ex back: uploading an iMovie photo montage of your vacation pictures to YouTube.com, set to Pat Benatar's "We Belong"; showing up at their house in a trench coat with nothing underneath; showing up at their office with a dozen roses and their name **tattooed** on your neck; standing outside their apartment holding a boom box over your head, playing Peter Gabriel's "In Your Eyes."

At the time, in your mind, these seem like really, *really* good ideas. The delusional hope is that your ex will think, "Oh, they're so clever/adorable/funny, how can I even *think* of dumping them?!" This works in romantic comedies. It does not work in real life. Usually because in real life, these "genius" ideas only come to you after six or seven shots of Jack with a P.B.R. chaser. Thus, their execution is sloppy, their message incoherent, and their deliverer (you)

→

sweaty, red-faced, and on the verge of passing out. Indeed, how can they resist? A.k.a. pathetic.

dial and dash

To call an ex and hang up immediately, or at least hang up after you listen to them say "Hello? . . . Hello? . . . Helllllloooooo?" If you have a shred of pride left, you will call from a blocked number. If you don't, you will call on your own phone so they will see your caller ID and at least be thinking about you.

disposable digits

Temporary phone numbers that forward calls to your real phone number or a voicemail box. In other words, full-body armor for daters who have the uncanny knack of converting every dumpee into a **bunny-boiler**. These numbers (available at sites like TossableDigits.com) are active only for as long as you want them to be, and are the perfect compromise between giving someone your real number and directing them to the **Rejection Hotline**. Let's say you meet a hottie at a bar and want to see them again, but aren't convinced that in your present (i.e. sozzled) state you can distinguish between boyfriend/girlfriend material and a bunny-boiler. Then give them a set of disposable digits—if it all goes belly-up, just trash that number and start over (without ever having to deal with the hassle of *actually* changing your number!). Note: We do not advocate using such digits to go **A.W.O.L.**; they

D

are merely an escape hatch for crazy-magnets. In addition, we are not responsible for what happens if the bar hottie turns out to be boyfriend/girlfriend material after all and you have to explain why you never gave them your real number ("You thought I was disposable?!??"). You *could* always maintain a set of disposable digits for the entire length of every relationship you enter into—but that little lie will eat away at the foundation of your relationship like a termite on steroids. See also **Dear John dot coms** and **emotional Imodium**.

doctor's note

A lame excuse to use for a breakup, unless it's true. If it *is* true, it's a **get-out-of-jail-free card**—after all, how can you argue with "My therapist thinks I need to focus on myself before I can take on a serious relationship," or "My shrink thinks you're wrong for me," or "I'm too depressed to date; I don't want to bring you down," or "I

have sociopathic tendencies." However, if you suspect your depressed dumper of totally faking, you are completely within your rights to ask for an actual signed note from the doctor.

downsized

Getting dumped by a coworker, or worse, your boss. If you don't actually get fired, it will feel like you have: you won't be able to concentrate or get anything done, you'll hide out in your cubicle to avoid awkward water-cooler run-ins with the ex, you'll be spending more than you're earning on **retail therapy** and supplies for **numbing the pain**, and, if your ex has any say in the matter, you'll be kept off projects that might be good for your career but are bad for your ex's mojo. As long as your ex isn't actually carrying out this last crime, try to remain professional; you made your office space when you started sneaking off to the supply closet, now you have to work in it. Resist the temptation

→

to log on to their computer after business hours and sabotage their presentation by absconding with their pie charts, or to "accidentally" send an office-wide memo about their small, smelly body parts. If, however, your ex is using their power to prevent you from fulfilling your professional potential, then by all means sic Human Resources on their ass.

drunken dialies

The late-night, under-the-influence, undeniable urge to call a recent ex and slur into the phone, "How's it going?" (if you're feeling "smooth" and "subtle") or "Can I come over?" (if you're not). These calls typically occur around closing time; if the recipient of the call is also in a location where closing time has just been announced, then the call is 99.7% likely to end in booty. If, on the other hand, the ex was woken up by the call, then it is only 57.6% likely to end in booty.

The drunken dialies are a rite of passage of breakups, especially in one's teens, twenties, and thirties (okay, *only* in one's teens, twenties, and thirties; after that, they're just plain depressing). If the breakup ranked low on the melodrama Richter scale and *neither* party appears to be depressed, suicidal, delusional, or armed, then any area **F.E.M.A.s** should feel no obligation to prevent **ex sex** from happening.

However, if the drunken call is likely to lead to some serious morning-after fallout, then F.E.M.A.s are advised to step in and distract the drunken dialer with a situation-appropriate

D

suggestion ("Hey! Let's order Domino's and have them deliver it to the bar!").

If you know that *your* fingers tend to go walkies in the aftermath of a breakup and after one too many shots and a couple of country tunes on the jukebox, then you need to select a designated dialer when you're sober. You should give this designated dialer prior permission to use any physical force necessary to confiscate your phone. By the way, a good citizen doesn't take this precaution only to protect their *own* "hand" after a breakup or during a **break**; it's considered a nice thing to do if your ex is the one suffering and is too weak to send your booty calls to voicemail.

On a final note, if you never got around to memorizing your ex's phone number, now would be a good time to delete their number from your mobile phone (see **cutting the cord**). If you can't bear to lose their digits altogether, write them down on a piece of paper and hide it in a place that you'll only be able to remember when sober.

dumping ground

See **chopping block**.

dumpster diving

❶ What **bottom-feeders** do.
❷ **Going through your neighbor's trash**.

E

emotional Imodium

What you need to take when you first start seeing someone so your hopes, your hormones, or the booze don't give you diarrhea of the mouth when it comes to whimsical, romantic feelings. The excited, nervous energy generated by a new crush is a feeling we all live for, but you must be judicious about laying on the charm at the beginning of a relationship. Otherwise, should there be an early breakup, it's made that much more confusing and painful for the dumpee by recent, spur-of-the-moment comments you might have made, such as "My therapist thinks you are perfect for me" or "I could really fall in love with someone like you" or "Will you be the mother/father of my children?" The grand faux pas of speaking too soon is the orgasm-inspired "I love you"

blurted out during sex at the end of your first date. Give it a couple of days: you'll realize that lust just looked an awful lot like love after those three martinis. See also **disposable digits**.

endgame

The intricate, symbiotic dance two people do around an inevitable breakup when they both know, without explicitly discussing it, that they're in the last throes of a dysfunctional relationship. Neither wants to be the dumper and look like a dick, and yet neither wants to stick around long enough to be the pitiful dumpee, either. You buy time, trying to figure out the best way to end things. Meanwhile, you push each other's buttons to force an argument, and focus on each other's annoying habits to strengthen your resolve. You are trapped in a kind of breakup limbo until one of you makes a move, or else the whole thing fizzles out until neither can pretend there's even a sliver of

→

love left between you. In this case (and this is the *only* case), a breakup *can* be **mutual**. If you endure a few months or years of this kind of endgame, then the breakup can be considered fair and balanced, no matter who "officially" pulls the trigger. We think this happened once, back in the seventies.

endship

❶ The imaginary friendship insincerely wished for out loud by a dumper during the breakup. A dumper without a backbone or any imagination relies upon a **cliché** such as "I hope we can still be friends" or "I think we would be better suited as friends" to get out of the entanglement, only to start erasing your digits from their cell phone 2.5 seconds after they've left you in a puddle on the floor. They will never write, never call, never even consider you for a position as a friend *with benefits*. When they see you out in public next, they will avoid eye contact like your face is the noonday sun.

Should you approach them, be prepared for an icy reception that will take you back to junior high when you tried to sit at the cool kids' table at lunch. You'll probably end up crying in the bathroom alone, again. ❷ The friendship offered at the end of an amicable breakup that never materializes because both parties have absolutely nothing in common without the sex.

e-spying

The various high-tech means of snooping on an ex, from the mild (the occasional **Google** search) to the invasive (logging in to their **online dating** profile →

or Hotmail account after making an educated guess as to their username and password) to the slightly psychotic (posing as a stranger on an online social networking site you know they frequent and luring them into a "casual" conversation about their dating life).

There are two issues at stake here: what you should and shouldn't do from an ethical standpoint, and what you should and shouldn't do in order to protect yourself from further heartache. Ethically, anything that's in the public domain is yours to look at, which gives you a free pass on all the Googling and **MySpace** gawking. But we hope we don't need to tell you that breaking into someone else's private correspondence or using a false identity to get someone to spill the beans is just plain wrong.

Besides, no good can come of digging this deep. If you find nothing, you'll feel icky, and if you find something, you'll feel a hell of a lot worse than icky. There are certain codes of etiquette that nice people abide by when it comes to breakups, and when you try to snoop your way into the **cold hard truth**, you undo all the good work they put in. Those **white lies** are for *your* benefit, remember? And so is **padding the fall**. So stay the hell away.

As far as Googling goes, we recommend waiting at least three months after a breakup before seeking them out online. It's certainly healthier than calling your ex "just to say hi" if you're supposed to be **cutting the cord**, but a bad search result could set you back a whole step in the **healing process**. If in doubt, ask your best friend if they think you're ready for the Google. And remember that like all guilty pleasures, Googling is best indulged in moderation: three hours a night for an entire month is not good for the soul. Besides, think how much better that time could be spent on your **breakover**! Here's a good rule of thumb: For every hour you spend Googling, force yourself to spend an hour working on your breakover online: tweaking your online dating profile,

E

replying to your latest "matches," working on that blog you've been meaning to launch for the past five years, adding mysterious and sexy new friends to your **MySpace** list just in case your ex decides to snoop on *you,* etc.

eternal return

A seemingly endless cycle of breaking up and getting back together experienced by a couple who can't live with each other, but can't live without each other either. Based on the philosophical concept most famously (or at least most recently) touted by Nietzsche, that the universe is composed of *finite* matter but *infinite* time (which is cyclical and not linear) and thus repeats itself eternally: we're forced (or doomed) to live our same lives over and over again. Kind of like Eminem and Kimberly Mathers or Pamela Anderson and Kid Rock. See also **groundhog dump**.

ex appeal

The sex appeal of exes. Once you break up, your ex suddenly becomes taboo, unattainable, out of reach—all qualities that are incredibly sexually attractive. Not having obstacles to overcome to have sex with each other was probably one of the reasons you broke up in the first place: After all, it's the challenge, the chase, that's half (if not more of) the fun. (Or so our A.D.D. keeps telling us.) You may also be suffering from **rose-colored hindsight**, a tendency to idealize your ex, post-breakup. And suddenly, all those things you took for granted about your partner become blatantly obvious; the three-course meals your ex cooked that you were growing tired of sound pretty good when your brand-new partner thinks fine dining is the upstairs window seats at McDonald's. Plus, there's something comforting about the idea of **returning to the well**: you're familiar with each other's bodies, you know how to get each other off, and

→

there will be no surprises, like an unexpected third nipple or a tail.

ex communication

❶ Closure (def. #1). **❷** What transpires between **frexes** with a high **ex factor**.

ex con

Swindling an ex by winning back their confidence, only to trick them into taking you back or to exact **revenge** on them. The former might be planned by a desperate ex who requests your audience for **closure** with promises of "no funny business," only to show up bearing flowers or wearing a revealing top; they'll proceed to order champagne and slip you a roofie for **second-chance sex**, and the next thing you know, they're in your apartment reinstalling their Oral-B in your toothbrush holder. In the latter

case, they may convince you that they'd like to be **frexes** or would simply like to engage in no-strings-attached sex, only to get you in a vulnerable position where they can either humiliate you or get you fired, arrested, or deported.

E

ex factor, the

The degree to which a person you're dating is connected to, hung up on, or friendly with their ex. For example, someone with a high ex factor may share custody of three kids with a very controlling ex-spouse. Or your partner may have only recently—and devastatingly—broken up and is still carrying around a lot of baggage from that relationship: pictures on the fridge from their last vacation, a pet Chihuahua they bought together that makes your partner cry every time it takes a shit, or actual baggage and luggage the ex left behind because your partner has more closet space. Or perhaps your partner is close friends, or **frexes**, with the ex, resulting in awkward social outings where stories are told about your partner and the ex that start "Remember that time we . . ." and recount apparently hi-lar-i-ous antics the two of them shared that leave all partygoers in stitches except you. If you are jealous, insecure, and petty—like most people with a pulse—then we highly recommend not getting serious about someone with a high ex factor.

ex sex

Returning to the well, blue binning, recycling, **closure** . . . whatever you call it, sex with an ex-boyfriend or -girlfriend is highly likely if one or more of the following criteria are met: ❶ The breakup was *not* a **post-traumatic stress dis**. ❷ Neither of you has a serious **someone else**. ❸ You try to remain friends (see **frexes**).

Even if you don't particularly care for one another, ex sex is *still* highly likely because the fools we mortals be are hardwired to want what we don't or can't have. For example, you meet up with your ex for an amicable drink, look across the table at them through the soft-focus lens of two dirty martinis, and look back on your relationship with **rose-colored hindsight**—suddenly their **ex appeal** goes through the roof! Next thing you know, your pants are around your ankles in the one-person co-ed bathroom of the bar, your hair is mussed, your breathing is heavy. you haven't had sex like this since the very first time you two did it together!

In the moment, ex sex is familiar, comfortable, and incredibly dramatic. Immediately

→

E

afterward is when things get awkward, uncomfortable, and annoying. *How* awkward, uncomfortable, or annoying depends entirely on the particular brand of ex sex you engaged in: the more ambitious the goal of the sex, the more likely your discomfort and disappointment. For example, pathetic **second-chance sex** (a.k.a. take-me-back sex) almost always ends in tears for the initiator. **Pageant sex**, intended to make your partner eat their heart out, is fairly lighthearted and empowering, no matter what the outcome: you feel like hot shit whether they ask you out again or not. **One for the road** sex engaged in immediately after a breakup will make walking out the door that much more painful, but hey, at least you had an orgasm. **Revenge sex** can be the most destructive of all forms of ex sex, damaging both the recipient (who may have just been tied up and given a reverse Mohawk) as well as the giver (who now has to live with themselves for the rest of their life knowing they

stooped to the low amoebas-on-fleas-on-rats level).

As with almost any kind of sex, ex sex is bound to stir up warm and fuzzy feelings in at least one of you, which means it's often a precursor to a **groundhog breakup** or the beginning of **eternal return**. The lucky few are able to turn ex sex into fun and meaningless booty calls between **friends with benefits**.

E

THE BEST MOVIE SCENE INVOLVING HOT DOG: GREA

DANNY ZUKO (JOHN TRAVOLTA) TRIES TO COP A FEEL WHILE SITTING IN HIS CONVERTIBLE AT THE DRIVE-IN WITH SANDY OLSSON (OLIVIA NEWTON-JOHN).

SANDY: "Danny!"

DANNY: "Sandy! Oh, Sandy."

SANDY: "What are you doing?"

DANNY: "Oh, Sandy. Don't worry about it. Nobody's watching."

SANDY: "Danny, get off me!"

DANNY: "Come on, Sandy, what's the matter with you? I thought I meant something to you."

SANDY: "Meant something to you! You think I'm going to stay here with you in this . . . this sin wagon? You can take this piece of tin!"

[*Throws his class ring at him and runs away.*]

DANNY: "Sandy, you just can't walk out of a drive-in."

E BREAKUP
NG A DANCING
SE (1978)

MUSICAL INTERLUDE: "Stranded at the drive-in/Branded a fool/What will they say/Monday at school?"

F

face-to-face imperative, the

There may be fifty ways to leave your lover, but your obligation, as a member of the dating pool and occasional caretaker of someone else's heart and loins, is to break up with someone *in person* if you've been together for more than a few weeks *or* you've had sex more than twice.

Over the years we've often been asked by prospective dumpers why we insist on this course of action. "Isn't it better for their pride if I don't witness their breakup-induced break-down?" they might ask. Or, "Won't they feel duped if I call to make a date only to dump them?" Or, "Isn't it just putting lipstick on a pig?" So here are our top five reasons why (see the **chopping block** entry for the where): ❶ It shows respect. It says that you take the matter seriously and are prepared to devote some time to the matter, rather than phoning it in before hitting the town. ❷ It sucks for you big-time (*way* worse than doing it over the phone). The dumpee's heart is breaking; it helps them a little to know you're feeling some pain, too. ❸ Your dumpee gets to wail and gnash their teeth in front of you and show you *exactly* what you're putting them through. (Again with the thing about you feeling some pain, too.) ❹ They get to plead their case. If you dump them over the phone, they'll be left thinking, "If only they could see what hot shit I am in these gold lamé leggings, they'd never be able to leave me." ❺ It saves them face. "Everyone knows" that you're "supposed" to dump someone in person. It's just the done thing. Because of this, the dumpee will feel doubly like a loser if you phone-dump them: not only do you never want to see them again, you don't even think they're worthy of a common courtesy.

If, on the other hand, you've had only a few great dates but you're just not feeling it, or you had a one-night stand where you mistakenly declared a desire to see them again, then a phone call or **Dear John**/Jane e-mail will suffice. It is commonly assumed that a phone call trumps an e-mail in this scenario, due to the simple fact that the call causes the dumper more pain (see #2 above). It's not a bad argument, but actually, if you think about it from the dumpee's point of view, an e-mail allows them to gape/stutter/weep in private. During a face-to-face breakup, all that drama is part of the process (see #3 above), but when a casual relationship is winding down, a little privacy is nice. Any wailing or gnashing of teeth would just make them come across as kinda weird, thereby adding to their humiliation. Whereas if you dump them via e-mail, they can take time to compose themselves and *then* compose their oh-so-breezy reply (or better yet, classify you, the sender, as "junk"). Whatever you do, avoid an **I.M. F.U.**–not only out of common human decency, but for your own protection as well.

Finally, the *only* situation in which a text-message dump is appropriate is if you receive an S.M.S. saying, "Great to meet you last night, wanna get together this weekend?" and your *honest* reply is, "Sorry, I don't remember. Who's this?" See also **Dear John dot coms, disposable digits**, and **wakaresase**.

F

faking it

Feigning broken-heartedness to get laid: you appear to need a shoulder to cry on, then you need a shoulder to drool on, then you need a shoulder to rub your genitals on. We're not sure which is worse, faking it or **bottom-feeding**—they're two sides of the same heinous coin. While someone who can fake it may not have a heart to begin with, we can only hope that someday karma comes back around with a chainsaw for a triple bypass.

faux hawks

People who **fake** heartbreak to get a **sympathy fuck**.

F.E.M.A.

Friendly Emergency Management Agent. A friend who will be by your side, call your ex **Fuckface**, take you out cruising, get you drunk, monitor your vital signs, etc. However, don't expect too much from your F.E.M.A., especially if they suffer from the **hetero Harry handicap**—and even if they don't, they may be too focused on their own dating dramas to deal with your basic post-breakup needs. A.k.a. the buddy system.

flirting therapy

Giving—and receiving—casual romantic/sexual attention as a distraction from the pain of a breakup. When you have fallen off the bike of love and you're feeling bruised and dirty and stupid-looking, you've got to get up, dust yourself off, wave to the onlookers, and get back on again. No need to go on any statewide bike-a-thons—just once around the block is enough to remind yourself that there are a lot of people to see and do in the world besides **Fuckface**.

At first you won't feel much like flirting, but it's like smiling: even if you're depressed, forcing yourself to smile can trick your brain into feeling better. So have a shot, go out with your buds, and let go. Buy someone a drink. Be a little touchy-feely, but keep it light: any contact should be short and sweet. Indulge in a little sexual innuendo (but only if you can tell the difference between witty, tongue-in-cheek innuendo and sleazy, psycho innuendo). The

F

most important aspect of all this tactile and emotional flirting is that it seem breezy, spur-of-the-moment, nonchalant, confident, meaningless, mindless, and goalless—even if it *feels* heavy, forced, deliberate, desperate, and ridiculous. It's easier to practice on people you're not seriously interested in. Remember, you're not flirting to get laid or find a new love. No, you're flirting because you're just a sexy, sexy person who deserves attention.

But you don't want to overdo it and risk leaving your own trail of broken hearts in your wake. Unfortunately, everyone's definition of flirting is different: what some people consider just being friendly, others consider hot and heavy sexual flirting. One man's handshake hello is another man's B.J. The point being, everything's open to interpretation, so have fun, but err on the side of caution. And no hitting on the one who has been crushing on you since the fifth grade, just to boost yourself up, when you know you'd rather eat bull testicles than go out with them.

As long as you are not malicious, dishonest, or thoroughly inconsiderate, you should make it around the block without knocking someone down. A.k.a. a pick-me-up.

foreclosure

Rejecting a dumpee's request for **closure**.

fortune cookie rule

You know how you're always supposed to add ". . . in bed" onto the end of the fortune that came in the cookie with your lo mein? Well, with breakup excuses, try adding ". . . with you" to see if the dumper's excuse/explanation makes more sense. For example, "I'm not ready for a relationship right now . . . with you." "**It's not you, it's me** . . . with you." "I'm too depressed . . . with you." If that just gives you the blues instead of giving you clarity, you could always try adding on "... in bed" instead, just to make yourself feel better. "It's just not working for me ... in bed." "You're great, I'm an idiot ... in bed." "I think we should just be friends ... in bed" (the ol' **booty bait 'n' switch**!).

I'M NOT READY FOR A RELATIONSHIP RIGHT NOW... WITH YOU

frexes

❶ Exes who are friends. Not to be confused with exes who are **fuck buddies**. There *have* been cases of exes having amicable, purely platonic relationships—it's rarer than digestion at a supermodel convention, but it happens. Certain factors make becoming frexes more likely:

letting a significant amount of time pass after the breakup before friendship initiation to let wounds heal and bygones be bygones; getting into new, satisfying relationships with people *not* in either of your social circles; if we're talking about hetero relationships, siding with Sally on the whole "Can men and women be friends?" debate; smoking pot; and possessing the mutant gene that predisposes you to such mature, rational relationships.

If the breakup wasn't exactly a **mutual decision** (when are they ever?) and you did the dumping with the **cliché** "Can we still be friends?" but actually *meant* it, then give your ex some time and space—you don't want them thinking you're getting in touch again to, well, get *in touch* again. Ideally you won't reconnect until they've gone on at least a few dates or had sex with another person. When you do talk, be honest and open. Ask them encouragingly if they've reposted their personal ad or if they've met anyone new, but be vague about

→

your own amorous pursuits. If you used the "I'm not ready" excuse with them, don't gush about your new significant other, the one who you think might be the One. And if you're really serious about being friends, then *don't* sleep with them. Not even once.

❷ That annoying breed of ex who hangs around your current partner just a little too often, who chums it up with all parties just a little too forcedly, like a gnat buzzing in your ear. It's an unfortunate side effect of being partnered with one of those highly evolved, emotionally mature people who is capable of such platonic, functional relationships with lovers past.

Dating someone with a high **ex factor** requires the patience and inner peace of the Dalai Lama. And while you may be the "considerate" type who doesn't subject your partner to your own exes, you shouldn't ask the same of your partner, any more than you should ask them to give up their best friend, their old yearbook that's inscribed with

syrupy messages from their junior high sweetheart, or their trusty vibrator/favorite porno—*especially* if you trust them (as any good partner should) and you aren't threatened by any of these frexes (like all good robots). We strongly advise against swatting—it's just a reflection of your own insecurities. Save your righteous outrage for matters that *really* bug you. As long as your partner isn't indulging in long walks on the beach at sunset with the ex, you can learn to handle it. Even if they're on good speaking terms, you can handle it. After all, proximity to an ex doesn't automatically mean your partner will accidentally fall on top of them in the missionary position again.

Just tell your partner that you feel a bit weird about it all and ask them to be sensitive to that. You certainly don't have to hang out with these exes during *every* social outing, but if this friendship is important to your partner, you gotta put in a little face time. Think of these

F

meetings as character-building, brownie-point-earning occasions for you. You want to find a happy medium between crazed possessiveness and robotic indifference: be polite, charming, friendly but not over-the-top BFF friendly, when you're out in public with these buggers; then feel free to playfully—we said *playfully*—talk shit about them with your partner in private, as a way to vent honestly, but also as a way to show you care enough to be just a smidge jealous. After all, let's be honest, jealousy is at least partially responsible for the "bothersome" effect these encounters have on us. Though some consider it a toxic, irrational emotion for unevolved heathens, jealousy is perfectly natural, and a pinch of it goes a long way, kind of like salt, cheesiness, and BDSM.

If it helps you to get through these annoying hangout sessions, you should feel free to privately indulge in smug feelings of being the conquering hero/ine. It would not even be inappropriate to imagine (once again, *privately*) that you're far superior in bed than any of your partner's past and present suitors; after all, you're the one your partner is fucking *now*. Who knows, by demonstrating such maturity (outwardly at least) and spreading world peace, some day you might even end up good friends with one of these losers.

friends with benefits

In the context of breakups, **frexes** who can occasionally call each other up for sex if neither is in a relationship. It's a kinder, gentler term than "**fuck buddy**" and usually applies to kinder, gentler people who broke up amicably and now have fun, lighthearted sex with lots of giggling.

frumping

Dumping a friend. "Friends are forever" makes a nice Hallmark card, but platonic peers can

→

grow apart or even grow to hate each other, just as some (many) lovers do. All relationships are complicated; simply taking sex out of the equation doesn't suddenly turn quantum physics into simple addition. Sure, it's a little less messy when you don't have to worry about pregnancy or STDs or soiling the sheets. But opportunities for miscommunication, betrayal, and disappointment abound even if you're not getting naked together. Or perhaps one of you grows up while the other stagnates in a puddle of their own crap—what once seemed like audacity, boldness, humor, or a hipster haircut turns out to be just cheapness, bigotry, meanspiritedness, or a mullet.

Whatever the cause, friendships might even be *more* delicate and vulnerable than romantic relationships precisely because you *don't* have getting naked together to fall back on. Without makeup sex to look forward to, forgiveness is a lot less appealing.

With romances, it's usually better to burn out in a blaze of fiery, face-to-face conflict; with friendships, however, it's better to fade away. In fact, it's the *only* way to frump someone. Unless they've betrayed or disappointed you in some egregious way that merits **the Talk**, or in this case, a talking to (e.g. stole your boyfriend/girlfriend, stole your favorite shirt, stole your identity à la *Single White Female*), then the best course of action when you find yourself severely annoyed or creeped out by a friend is to gradually but steadily pull away: your response time to their e-mails, calls, and texts should increase geometrically until you simply stop responding altogether. It may sound harsh, but it's infinitely better than trying to explain to this person that even though you're "allowed" to have as many friends as you can keep track of on **MySpace**—unlike with monogamous dating, where you have to pick just one—you simply can't be bothered with their particular brand of friendship. With the gradual pullout, they can at least pretend that you two simply grew apart, not by choice but by inconvenient circumstances: too much work, too much geographic distance, etc. (Hell, you can even convince *yourself* of that if it makes you feel better about the frump.) Of course, if you've got a **leg-clinger** for a friend who couldn't take a hint even if they were playing Clue, then you may need to resort to the **cold hard truth**. Tread lightly: **bunny-boilers** aren't just jilted lovers; they're dissed friends, too. See also **frexes**.

fuck buddy

Someone with whom you once had a serious love/hate relationship and with whom you *now* have a purely sexual love/hate relationship, one that's based on animosity and incredibly hot anal sex. Unlike a **friend with benefits**, you would not call this person just to talk if you got fired or your cat got run over, though you could probably hit them up for a loan if you were in a bind. However, the fact that the sex is usually

naughtier (think: hair-pulling, name-calling, spanking) more than makes up for the lack of emotional connection.

fuck 'n' chuck

❶ A heinous postcoital dump, the likes of which would have been right at home in the plotline of *In the Company of Men.* It's basically the groin kick of the breakup world, most often perpetrated by scumbags who lead people on with talk of a future together and promises of eternal devotion just to get into the future dumpee's pants. The longer the pursuit, the

→

more heinous the crime. For instance, if you know that (a) your partner is waiting until it's "the right time" to have sex with you and (b) there is no way in hell you'd ever consider a real relationship with them, and yet you continue to stick it out simply to sample the merchandise, then you should be strung up by your balls (let's be honest—fuck 'n' chucks are a mostly male-perpetrated phenomenon). This is how **bunny-boilers** are created.

When a fuck 'n' chuck is committed as part of a **post-traumatic stress dis** (because the dumpee cheated on you or screened your homemade sex tape at the frat/sorority house), it usually takes the form of a **mid-sesh smackdown** (because, really, why should they get the satisfaction of orgasming?). But if you want to score one more orgasm for yourself before hitting the road, try breaking out this line right after your happy ending: "*Now* I remember what I meant to do today: Break up with you!" A.k.a. hump 'n' dump, barbarian breakup (named for

Conan the Barbarian, who famously "dumped" a woman by throwing her into the fire immediately after humping her; she *was* a witch, but still . . . that's harsh, dude).

❷ An utterly *charming* term for a one-night stand. When you think about it, a one-night stand is, for all intents and purposes, a whirlwind romance, mini-relationship, and **Band-Aid break** all rolled up in one. And just as the final act of a full-blown relationship should be tailored to the kind of relationship that came before it, so your post-sex obligations correlate directly to the expectations you raised the night before. If you wooed your one-nighter to bed with promises of Central Park picnics and weekends in the Hamptons, then you are obliged to follow through (and if you don't, you're a scumbag who deserves to be hung up by your genitals. . . . See def. #1). But if you can honestly say that you made no false promises in order to close the deal (hooray for you, upstanding citizen) then you are required, simply,

F

to be polite. If the liaison takes place at your own apartment, let them stay the night (unless they live in easy walking distance), offer them coffee and toast (no eggs Benedict) in the morning, but don't dilly-dally in your effort to get to that place you "need to be" the next day. If the tryst is at their place and you wish to depart, engage in light caressing and conversation for at least twenty minutes (no spooning or swapping intimate childhood memories). But then confess that you don't sleep well away from home—plus, you have to get up early tomorrow. If you decide to sneak out at 5:00 A.M. instead, then leave a cheeky "you were great last night" note on a Post-it or napkin (See **Dear John**). Don't ask for a phone number if you have no intention of dialing it, and don't leave yours if you plan on "accidentally" making the "6" look like a "0." If they attempt to give you their digits (by, say, scrawling them on your palm while you sleep), do your best to avoid the meaningless "**I'll call you**" closer. How about a

more honest quick kiss and "goodbye" instead? Your final obligation is to act like an adult next time you see them— be friendly, ask how they're doing, smile mischievously in a way that acknowledges the earlier dalliance without having to actually speak of it. Whatever you do, don't hide under the table.

Fuckface

Most common nickname for an ex who has broken one's heart. Invaluable to the third step of the **healing process**: **thinking negatively**.

fucksimile

A person you sleep with solely because they remind you of your ex, either because you miss them like crazy and think that if you dim the lights, the spooning just might feel the same, or because you're craving proxy revenge and think that sneaking out the next morning without leaving your phone number will heal your wounds (it won't; it'll just make you feel like an even bigger loser). In some cases, pursuing a fuck-simile is a subconscious decision: you may not even realize the resemblance until your friends point it out over brunch the following morning. See also **rebound sex**.

me," like you're about to admit to having cancer or a tail, is utterly condescending. Any self-respecting dumpee would reply "Who fucking cares?" whether they mean it or not. And if they don't have the emotional forti-tude to fake it, well then you're just going to have another melt-down on your hands. Smooth move, Ex-Lax.

full disclosure

Letting a recent ex (or one who still has feelings for you) know that you're hooking up with someone new so they don't have to hear it from a third party (friends, **MySpace**, *US Weekly* magazine, etc.). While the intention to spare your ex pain and humiliation is noble, nine times out of ten, fessing up to a new affair to their face is more painful and humiliat-ing (for both of you!). Sitting them down for yet *another* seri-ous **Talk**, taking a deep breath, looking solemnly into their eyes, and saying, "There's some-thing you should know about

THE MOST SE[I]
BREAKUP SCE[N]
CASABLANCA.

RICK BLAINE [HUMPHREY BOGART]: "Inside of us, we both know you belong with Victor. You're part of his work, the thing that keeps him going. If that plane leaves the ground and you're not with him, you'll regret it. Maybe not today. Maybe not tomorrow, but soon and for the rest of your life."

ILSA LUND [INGRID BERGMAN]: "But what about us?"

RICK: "We'll always have Paris. We didn't have, we, we lost it until you came to Casablanca. We got it back last night."

ILSA: "When I said I would never leave you . . ."

RICK: "And you never will. But I've got a job to do, too. Where I'm going, you can't follow. What I've got to do, you can't be any part of. Ilsa, I'm no good at being noble, but it doesn't take much to see that the problems of three little people don't amount to a hill of beans in this crazy world. Someday you'll understand that. Now, now . . . Here's looking at you, kid."

2)

G

get-out-of-jail-free cards

Breakup lines that are definitive but not overly devastating, i.e. the dumpee won't take it too personally, they won't be able to argue their case, and they might not cry too much either. Note: These cards can only be whipped out when the line is actually *true*. And even if the line is true, the card may be considered invalid after more than six months of dating. But for medium-term relationships, where the **face-to-face imperative** is in play but china patterns haven't yet been discussed, the following lines may facilitate a brief and graceful exit: ❶ "You're great, but I'm still not over my ex" (i.e. it's *really* not you; this breakup was set in motion before I ever laid eyes on you). Qualifier: This line will go over only if you've been dating a very short while, your partner knows that you recently suffered a traumatic breakup, *and* they have an empathy streak a mile wide. ❷ "My dad just died and I need to heal alone." ❸ "I just realized I'm in love with my best friend whom I've known since we played in the sandbox together and whom everyone told me I would eventually marry, though I didn't believe them until now." Qualifier: This can only be used after a first date. ❹ "I think I might be gay/straight" (whichever one your partner *isn't*). ❺ "I just realized I'm a top/bottom" (whichever one your partner *is*). ❻ "My shrink has excused me from all relationship activities" (see **doctor's note**).

git 'er done

Step four of the breakup **healing process** for dumpees, this is when you channel the spirit of (a pre-prison jumpsuit) Martha Stewart and get productive. Think of it as distraction therapy with a bonus side effect of self-improvement. At this

→

point in your romantic career, change is your friend. Woody Allen once said that a relationship is like a shark: If it's not constantly moving forward, it dies. (See page 172.) But if you spent the past year or three making sure that your *relationship* was moving forward, chances are you neglected other aspects of your life that should also be constantly moving forward: career, hobbies, interior decorating, etc.

You don't have to shave your head, join the Peace Corps, and renounce IKEA to enjoy the benefits of change. Below are a few small suggestions to help add new excitement to your life, make every ordinary moment extraordinary, and make over your life! (In a past life this book was a self-help best-seller. Hey, who moved our cheese?) Do any or all of the following. Repeat as necessary.
❶ Regarding your career: Ask for a raise. Demand a promotion. Send a memo. Redefine your role at the company. Take long lunches. Put whoopee cushions on your coworkers' chairs to enliven the working environment. Start your own company. Update your resume. Get a headhunter. Go on interviews. Network. Think outside the box. Quit. Get a new job that you care about. With cuter coworkers. ❷ Regarding your living arrangements: Get your own place or kick out your roommates. Redecorate. Paint the walls. Hire a feng shui consultant to optimize the energy in your bedroom. Browse flea markets. Remove *one* piece of IKEA furniture from each room. ❸ Regarding your hobbies: Learn how to play the guitar and compose cheesy songs about heartache and loss. Dig up your two-year-old to-do list and start attacking it. Read ***Anna Karenina***. Travel. Take a cooking class. Buy a book on the art of sensual massage. Make a short independent film. Make a five-year plan. Write a memoir, a screenplay, or the great American novel. Take up oil painting or photography. Add up your frequent flier miles for a free vacation. ❹ Regarding your relationships: Your *other*

G

relationships, we mean—you remember, all the people in your life *besides* your One and Only? Hopefully they remember you, too—but if romantic relationships tend to sweep you off like Dorothy to Oz, then now's the time to make amends with friends and family. Throw a dinner party. Organize a ladies'/boys' night out. Organize a family reunion. Build a family-tree Web site. Buy toilet paper without waiting for your roommate to nag you to. Add your siblings to your **MySpace** friends list. Visit your mom.

G

giving back to the community

❶ Volunteer work, activism, acts of charity, or just random acts of kindness as breakup therapy—this is stage five of the **healing process**. You do remember what community is, right? When even your best friend starts to tire of your breakup blues ("Snookums and I *always* used to watch *America's Next Top Model* together"), it might be time to reach out and touch someone in a whole new kind of way. So play bingo at the old folks' home. Become an environmental activist. Educate yourself about local politics—and actually vote. Give up booze for a month and donate the money you save to your favorite charity. Go though your closet and donate anything you haven't worn in more than twelve months (and get a receipt—it doesn't diminish the good deed to use it as a tax deduction!). This kind of therapy is not only great for your community—to say nothing of the personal

→

karma points—but it also puts your own problems into perspective. Nothing says "Suck it up, you pathetic, self-involved, spoiled brat" better than building a home for someone who got dumped because they contracted some rare, incurable disease and were left penniless with three hungry kids. ❷ Making yourself available to someone who just got dumped and is in serious need of a **sympathy fuck**.

goalie, playing

The debate-team strategy employed by a dumpee to point out flaws in their dumper's breakup argument as grounds for staying together. It's a common response to most **overcompensations**, some **big fat lies**, and a few **clichés**. For instance, when you tell someone, "My life is just too crazy right now" or "'I met you at the wrong point in my life," your dumpee won't consider that definite and irrefutable. Their brain will immediately

spin those comments to mean, "But someday, when I have it all under control, we'll be together again. I'll be thinking of you longingly until then. . . ." And they will either try desperately to convince you then and there that you're denying your true feelings, forcing you to resort to the **cold hard truth** in your own desperate attempt to extricate yourself from the relationship, *or* they will keep their fingers in your puddin' indefinitely: e-mailing, texting, and calling you regularly just to check in, to see "how you're doing" (read: "Are you ready to get back together yet????").

Alternatively, if you lay it on too thick—"You're the most wonderful person I've ever met"—you might get a sarcastic and embarrassing (for you) response: "Really? Is that right? Then why are you dumping me, you dumbass?" Insincerity is salt on their wound. And if they *don't* see through your insincerity, you could be in even deeper trouble: Overstating your feelings for the dumpee during the breakup may lead them to, say,

G

book an appointment with a couples counselor even though you only dated for two months. Oh, it's happened. When doing the dumping, your best bet is some variation of the definitive "We're just not right for each other." No need to add any hurtful specifics ("because I want someone more attractive/ambitious/independent/whatever"). With clarity and conviction, you won't be stringing along a dumpee, creating false hope and thus inviting late-night booze-fueled surprise visits from them. See also **non-committal breakup**.

I'm not ready for a relationship

going through your neighbor's trash

Asking out a close friend's ex. For the sake of simplicity, good karma, and world peace, don't ever do this. While crushes are often fleeting, friendships have the potential to last a lifetime. Is it worth risking that kind of long-term support and companionship for what will probably be a forgettable roll in the hay? There are millions of single people in this country! You have other options. However, if you suspect this could be a rare case of Romeo and Juliet (or Romeo and Julio, etc.) true love with serious marriage and baby potential (sans the dual suicide), then there are exceptions to the don't-ask rule, under certain circumstances: ❶ If you've gently, considerately, and sensitively discussed your honest, uncontrollable feelings of love for the ex with your friend and they've given you their sincere blessing. ❷ If your friend has moved on and is in a wholly

→

satisfying, happy, healthy relationship that makes their previous relationship with the ex look like a stint at Guantánamo. your friend won't hate you; they'll just feel sorry for you for settling for second best. ❸ If the statute of limitations has passed on your friend's right to be possessive about the ex. To calculate that figure, use the following formula: ([length of relationship in months] X 1.75) + 2 months, with a cap at 2 years. For instance, if your friend seriously dated the ex for nine months, then you can make your move just under a year and a half after the breakup—giving your friend a courteous heads-up first, of course. ❹ If your friend is friendly with the ex, but not *too* friendly. Ideally, you want your friend to believe the ex is a genuinely good person who deserves happiness (perhaps your friend now sets up the ex with coworkers). But if your friend thinks (hopes) there's even the slightest chance they'll get back together, or else believes the ex truly is

Satan, then take a cold shower and put up a personal on Match.com. ❺ If you are willing to lose the friend for good. Because no matter how much therapy they've received, your friend is likely to feel hurt, jealous, betrayed, and a little weirded out, even if they don't admit it. A.k.a. uncool.

Google

The tool that turns every scorned lover into a private dick. Google is the reason you know that your ex (a) finally lost the battle with their receding hairline; (b) just published a cat training manual that's out-selling your self-help tome on Amazon.com by two to one; (c) is now dating someone younger, hotter, and more successful than you; (d) is now gay; (e) is now dating their right hand (assuming your ex is one of those narcissistic bloggers who recounts the minutiae of their every waking moment); or (f) just had a small airport named after them. As

G

you can see, Google is a mixed bag that should be handled with care. If you're not sure you can handle the **cold hard truth**, then log on to eBay and shop for some new trinkets instead. Google searches are best reserved for distant exes, so that unpleasant results (Nobel awards, etc.) can be quickly shrugged off with an emergency **therapy fuck**, and more pleasing results (plastic surgery mishaps, etc.) can be enjoyed with a private moment of schadenfreude. See also **e-spying**.

groundhog dump

When a **noncommittal breakup** is dragged out over the course of multiple days or weeks, so the poor dumpee is forced to relive the same damn breakup all over again.

hairstylist cut

Breaking up with the person who cuts your hair because you've found **someone else**. While you may have discussed the intimate details of your last colonoscopy with your stylist, he or she is still a business associate, *not* a lover. Thus, do not humiliate them (or yourself) by sitting them down for **the Talk**. Treat this as a **frumping**, and simply disappear. If things don't work out with your new barber and you go crawling back to your old flame, you may come up with a little **white lie** about where you got the new warm highlights: perhaps you were on a month-long business trip, had a bad hair day, and panicked. Or maybe your stylist friend from L.A. was in town and insisted on giving you a freebie. However, if they suspect you of fibbing, be warned: you may end up with a Flock of Seagulls haircut.

hate fucking

❶ Sleeping with the enemy—not your ex's nemesis or family relations (see **revenge fuck** for that) but your ex. **Ex sex** isn't always a strategy to win someone back or a **sympathy fuck**; sometimes it's a case of "I hate you so much I could come." Not recommended more than once per breakup, hate fucking works best when a relationship ends in a massive screaming match that leads to a bout of hair-pulling, back-scratching, hot-as-balls rutting. No spooning necessary. **❷ Revenge fucking**.

healing process, the

❶ Numb the pain.
❷ Cut the cord.
❸ Think negatively and avoid **rose-colored hindsight**.
❹ Git 'er done.
❺ Give back to the community.
❻ Get a **breakover**.
❼ Mark the occasion.
❽ Engage in **retail therapy**.
❾ Go on the **rebound**.
❿ Think positively. See also "How to Get Over a Breakup (in Ten Easy Steps)" (page 7), and each entry listed above, for more details.

hetero Harry handicap

The inability of a heterosexual man's straight male friends to eat ice cream with him post-breakup while blowing sunshine up his ass, such as "What-*ev*-ahh, she was so not your type. You are so hot! I wish I had your hair"—thus resulting in a longer, lonelier, more painful recovery process for said man.

high fidelity

A reconstruction of your past breakups, achieved by paying a friendly visit to all your previous exes, as a means of gaining perspective on a current breakup. From the Nick Hornby novel and John Cusack vehicle of the same name. If you do actually gain some perspective, then you have achieved high fidelity.

I'll call you

Meaningless drivel, whether it's uttered by your one-night stand (see **fuck 'n' chuck**, def. #2), your online-personals blind date (see **online offing**), or your **frex**. If someone says "I'll call you," just assume they won't until they do. Try not to take this personally—people don't mean to lie. It's just that these three little words have become something of a social tic, blurted out in the awkward lull at the end of a conversation. It's not polite, though it's intended to be. Yes, life would be grand if we could all agree to actually call when we say we will, but that's as likely to happen as people suddenly letting subway riders exit the cars before piling in themselves. No, the best we can do is agree that "I'll call you" means absolutely nothing. So stop with the self-comforting excuses ("she probably lost my number"; "he must have been abducted by aliens") and move on.

The platonic business/acquaintance equivalent of the romance world's "I'll call you" is "Let's have lunch." It's a punctuation mark, not an action point, so best to brown-bag it. And if someone says "Let's *do* lunch"? Here's hoping they never call, for who would want to digest food with such a boor?

I will survive

❶ Rousing motto for the recently dumped. Did they think you'd crumble? Did they think you'd lay down and die? Oh no, not you! You will survive, and not only that, you will get a **breakover** that will make your ex drool. Now you'll hold your head up high and they'll see you, somebody new (thanks, breakup body!), not that chained-up little person still in love with them. ❷ Gloria Gaynor's '70s disco hit, guaranteed to cause every straight man in earshot to go scuttling for cover (and a refill) and any woman who has

been dumped in the past decade to sprint to the dance floor, dragging her more recently dumped friend by the hand. We don't care if you hate the song; you still have to hit the dance floor. You do it for every woman who's ever been dumped, anywhere. We didn't make the rule, but damn it, we *will* enforce it.

I.M. F.U.s

❶ Dumping someone via instant messaging. I.M. breakups are too loaded for our liking. What are you going to do, dump someone over I.M. and then stay logged on for the next three hours? That's like breaking up with someone and then carrying on drinking at opposite ends of the same bar. It's bound to lead to a dragged-out, open-ended, messy conversation. (Just when you think it's over, another "But WHY?!!!???" message pops up on your screen.) But if you log off immediately after doing the deed, then your dumpee will be forced to assume that you're rushing out the door for a date. I.M. F.U.s are an even worse idea for more casual breakups. First of all, what are you doing giving out your I.M. handle to someone you're not even going steady with? Do you really want your two-week fling to be alerted the second you log on or off your computer? Boundaries, people! See also **face-to-face imperative**.

❷ Breaking off an individual instant messaging session. Sometimes, trying to get out of an ongoing chat session without being rude can be as difficult and awkward as ending a two-year relationship. It's for this very reason that you should be more uptight than the club du jour's doorman when it comes to giving out your I.M. handle. Think about it: How many people do you want to be able to tap in to a direct, unfiltered connection with you? The judicious I.M.er shares this information only with people he or she has a high comfort level with, so that a simple "can't talk, coming down" (or a simple drop-off in the middle of a conversation) does not give offense. Of course, "judicious" and "I.M." rarely appear in the same sentence. If you find yourself trapped in an I.M. exchange, a bald-faced lie may be necessary, such as "Here comes my boss—gotta go!" or "Phone is ringing—talk to you later!" If you'd rather take a more honest approach, try a simple "Well, it's been great chatting, but I really should get back to work." Finally, you could experiment with the harsh-truth-couched-in-humor approach: "I'd love to keep chatting, but my TiVo is a jealous and demanding lover." If all this I.M. rebuffing becomes too much for you, then start over with a new handle, a blank buddy list, and a virtual velvet-rope policy.

I

impulse buy

A new boyfriend or girlfriend acquired by a dumpee on a whim, soon (i.e. *too* soon) after a bad breakup. You've got so much love inside you, burning a hole in your heart, you just want to spend it on somebody. So you go out on the town, trying to **numb the pain** with booze and reckless **flirting**, and in the process you meet someone who expresses an iota of interest in you. As far as they know, you're perfect; they have yet to be disappointed or annoyed by the fact that you leave pubic hair on the soap, that you hate your job but refuse to get a new one, or that you are addicted to The Sims. And they seem so cute and charming, you've just *got* to have them. After all, you think, they'll fill up this hole eating away inside you (they might even fill up other holes, if you're lucky). So you get swept up in the moment: you pick up someone you don't really need, only to realize a few days later (if not sooner) that you don't really want them,

either. Distract yourself from impulse shopping with a temporary bout of **celibacy** or a manic **git 'er done** period.

inconvenient truths

When you both like each other and things are going fine, but extenuating circumstances make the relationship unrealistic or impossible: you both just graduated high school and are going to different colleges, one of you is moving to Japan indefinitely, your respective religions don't allow interfaith marriage, one of you is a liberal environmental activist and the other is a neo-conservative who doesn't believe that the science is "in" on global warming yet. . . . Nothing personal, really; it's just not going to work out.

insanity, permanent

❶ The emotional state of your ex that led to you breaking up with them. ❷ The emotional state of your ex that led to them breaking up with you. ❸ Your emotional state that led to your ex breaking up with you.

insanity, temporary

The short-term period of mental instability that afflicts many of the recently dumped, especially those who feel the breakup was unjust. Crazy but fairly benign behavior includes crying uncontrollably at the super-market; rocking back and forth in an empty room à la Demi in *St. Elmo's Fire*; having visions of your ex in your bed beside you, cooking you dinner, or talking to you while you watch TV (and you talking back). Nuttiness akin to **revenge** and bordering on **bunny-boiler** behavior includes knifing every item of clothing in your ex's closet; burning their toothbrush and e-mailing them a photo of it in flames; stealing the left shoe from every pair they own (works particularly well on women who were more into their shoes than they were into you); opening a can of tuna and hiding it under their sofa cushion, etc. Needless to say, *private* temporary insanity is far more healthy than public acts of insanity, which may get you ostracized from your community of mutual friends, arrested, or committed.

I

issues

What you have in a relationship, especially immediately prior to a breakup. After the breakup, all those issues immediately convert into "baggage."

it's not you, it's me

The biggest **cliché** in the breakup book. We don't care how "true" this sentiment feels to you; there's no freakin' way you can use these five words in this order. That's like being dumped with a jingle! If you really feel that it's all "you," then find your own special way of conveying that. Perhaps, "I'm just not at the same place in my life that you are. I admire all that you've accomplished and how certain you are of what you want, but I'm just not there right now." Or—oh, forget it. This is supposed to be your *own* words, remember? Just make sure you don't accidentally veer into **cold hard truth** territory, such as, "It's not that you're not attractive enough, it's just that I'm so picky."

J

just looking

When you're sick of crying into your TV dinner at home and are ready to hit the town for some **flirting therapy**, but you know that actually following through on **rebound sex** would be disastrous (where "disastrous" means asking your one-night-stander to don a pair of your ex's used undies that you've been carrying around in your backpack for the past month, and then saying "hold me").

J

TRUEST-TO-L
MOUTH DIALO
BREAKUP SCE

ANNA (JULIA ROBERTS) TELLS HER HUSBAND LARRY (CLIVE OWEN) THAT SHE'S
LEAVING HIM FOR DAN (JUDE LAW); SHE'S JUST ADMITTED TO SLEEPING WITH DAN
EARLIER THAT EVENING IN THE APARTMENT SHE SHARES WITH LARRY.

LARRY: "Did you come?"

ANNA: "Why are you doing this?"

LARRY: "'Cause I want to know."

ANNA: "First he went down on me, and then we fucked."

LARRY: "Who was where?"

ANNA: "I was on top, then he fucked me from behind."

LARRY: "And that's when you came the second time."

ANNA: "Why is the sex so important?"

LARRY: "Because I'm a fucking caveman! . . . Did you
touch yourself while he fucked you?"

ANNA: "Yes."

LARRY: "You wank for him."

ANNA: "Sometimes."

LARRY: "And he does."

ANNA: "We do everything that people who have sex do!"

LARRY: "You enjoy sucking him off."

ANNA: "Yes!"

LARRY: "You like his cock."

ANNA: "I love his cock!"

LARRY: "You like him coming in your face."

ANNA: "Yes!"

LARRY: "What does it taste like?"

ANNA: "It tastes like you, but sweeter!"

LARRY: "That's the spirit. Thank you. Thank you for your honesty. Now fuck off and die, you fucked-up slag."

L

last supper, the

Getting dumped over dinner. This is not a spur-of-the-moment breakup resulting from a heated fight over pesto gnocchi, but a planned ax at the **Chopping Block** Café. If you're the dumper, avoid this move when possible, because we can't think which is worse: being dumped right after you've placed your order and feeling trapped until the check arrives, or being dumped over dessert and it slowly dawning on you that your partner just sat there and watched you eat your last meal on relationship death row. Plus, why burden the waitstaff, who are left wondering whether they're supposed to wait for the guest at table nine to stop bawling before clearing the plates? Besides, a dumpee *always* loses their appetite right after hearing the bad news, whereas a dumper, relieved at finally having delivered the message, often regains theirs suddenly. Nothing reminds the wretched dumpee how little they'll be missed quite like watching their dumper scarf down a jumbo burrito while their own stomach churns.

leg-clinger

A dumpee who cries, begs, and pleads with you to reconsider and take them back, practically holding on to one of your legs while you try to walk out the door. They reel off the lyrics of various breakup songs in desperation: "Don't leave me this way," "I can't live without you," and "Don't walk away" (see

"Dumping Ditties," page 186). Leg-clingers may also write looooong, law brief–type letters stating their case for why you two belong together, or resort to **desperate measures** to win you back (e.g. serenading you beneath your apartment window, getting your name tattooed on their ass, etc.) or simply stalk you. Treat leg-clingers firmly but delicately, because the unstable ones are only one rabbit's foot away from becoming full-blown **bunny-boilers**. Famous leg-clingers include Madame de Tourvel in *Les Liaisons Dangereuses/ Dangerous Liaisons/Valmont,* Scarlett O'Hara in *Gone with the Wind,* and Dan (Jude Law's character) in *Closer.*

librarian, pulling a

The cowardly act of dumping someone in a very public and quiet place so that they can't totally freak out on you. In extreme cases (or in college), this might be done in an actual library—perhaps in the self-help section—where every stifled whimper or cry of "You need *space*?!!!" will be greeted with an officious *shhhhhhhhh.* More commonly, though, the dumper will select a chilled-out restaurant or a sophisticated bar known for its stringent "keep it down" noise policy. While not quite as low-down lame as **pulling a Shannen**, the librarian move is nevertheless cheating the dumpee out of the scene that is rightfully theirs. Besides, the move may backfire if the dumpee insists on "getting some air" and then, once safely on the sidewalk, lays into you with thirty minutes of pent-up rage. It's not a pretty sight. See also **chopping block**.

looking as bad as you feel

A post-breakup decline in appearance and personal health—rise in cholesterol, dulling hair and skin, weight gain, etc.—due to excessive TV-watching, binge-drinking, binge-eating, chain-smoking, chain-bonging, etc. Often the result of allowing step 1 of the **healing process**, i.e. **numbing the pain**, to go on longer than the recommended one-to-two-week dosage. While it may feel good in the moment, the cumulative effects of abusing yourself in this way will only compound the depressive effect of the breakup. Antonyms: **breakover**, **Breakup Barbie**/Ken.

lost property

Unrecoverable personal items, either because you're the dumper and you know it's just not polite to ask, or you're the dumpee and you kind of either (a) like the fact that a little piece of you is still sitting in a crumpled pile in the corner of your ex's bedroom, or (b) like the fact that a little piece of your ex (e.g. their high-definition plasma TV) is still sitting in the corner of your living room. See also **booty haul**.

lying under oath

Pretending to leave the city/state/country to make for a smooth and ironclad breakup speech, or faking your own death as a means of going **A.W.O.L.** See also **big fat lies**.

M

marking the occasion

Changing your appearance in a significant, perhaps permanent, way, as step 7 of the post-breakup **healing process** for the dumpee. Do it as a sort of "X marks the spot" to denote the moment you exited the **mourning period** and began the recovery process.

For particularly traumatic breakups experienced by people with multiple tattoos, we recommend getting another tattoo: it's a little *self*-inflicted pain after all the heartbreak you had no say in, to help exorcise the breakup demons. It marks your body as your own, and the moment as a new beginning, a better chapter of your life. And its permanence reminds you that there's no turning back. (We've even heard stories of post-breakup branding, but your mom would never forgive

us if we gave a thumbs-up to that.) The tattoo shouldn't be about the breakup, of course—chances are, you'll grow to regret a "Talk to the hand, **Fuckface**" tattoo, just as Eminem will surely rue his "Kim: Rot in Pieces" tat—but rather, something that's all about *you*. That's the whole point, remember? You're moving *on*.

If you're not the inking type, piercings (ear, nose, nip, penis, clit) are all similarly painful and thus appropriate options, too. Or how about a flogging from a professional dominant/dominatrix to beat the sorrow out of you? For something a little more peaceful, try acupuncture.

If anything with needles or pain is about as appealing to you as getting dumped in the first place, then consider a new haircut instead. However, make sure you take a stylish friend along to guide the process, and choose a hairdresser you'd trust with your life. Nothing throws off the recovery process quite like an accidental bowl cut.

→

If bad hair days are the kind of thing that keep you up at night, then you might want to consider marking the occasion with some light pampering instead: a full-body massage, say, or a mani-pedi-facial day at the spa (they're all unisex indulgences these days, so enjoy!). See also **breakover**.

masturbation

Loving yourself when nobody else will. Masturbation is an important recovery tool for the dumpee (it's part of step 9 in the **healing process**), and way more healthy than simply **numbing the pain** (though we suppose if you indulge *excessively,* you might end up numbing body parts). For instance, drowning your sorrows in casual sex makes an innocent bystander an unwitting character in your tragedy. But with self-love, you can be selfish, you don't have to remember whose name to say, you don't have to worry about birth control or STDs, you're cheap and easy (unlike most potential sex partners), and you're a sure thing. Going out trolling for free sex to then be rejected *again* will only compound the pain.

Besides, letting your fingers do the walking can help relieve stress and tension. And the body's natural opiates that are released during orgasm can be a natural antidepressant. Sure, the oxytocin that is also released might make you long for a post-O cuddle, but that's fleeting. The positive effects of regular masturbation are long-term.

At first, getting yourself off solo may seem like a lonely endeavor. But think of it as simply training yourself for

→

bigger things to, um, come: it's like foreplay for your next relationship. For women, being your own sexual agent will give you confidence the next time you're entertaining guests in your bedroom ("I turn myself on all the time, so I know I can turn my partner on"). Knowing what you like and how to get it will make for better partner sex when you have it. And for everyone, a period of onanism will provide independence ("I'm with this person by choice, not sexual necessity"), and make you more protective of your parts ("I love my genitals too much to put them at risk by not practicing safe sex"). So go ahead and rub one out—eventually, it'll help put the sex you had with **Fuckface** to shame.

How do you make it feel less lonely in practice? Unfortunately, circle jerks went out with shoulder pads (though if leg warmers can make a comeback . . .). Instead, think of your self-love sessions as an evening (or just a few minutes) of well-deserved self-indulgence—kind of like getting a massage (with or without

a happy ending), ordering a pizza with the works just for yourself, and watching HBO. In fact, those activities are not only good post-breakup pampering, but pretty decent D.I.Y. foreplay for masturbation. And give your imagination a boost with an erotic (read: porno) book, movie, Web site, or soundtrack, so you're not tempted to think about dying alone in the middle of diddling. See also **celibacy** for more good reasons to go on a diet based exclusively on self-love.

Let's get it on...

match point

The precise moment in a breakup-in-progress when you say something like, "Well, for the record, I always thought your penis was too small" or "I lied: Your butt does look big in those pants"—in other words, something that can never be taken back and that guarantees that there will be no reconciliation, no **closure** get-together, and probably no **ex sex** either. Even if the thing said was a total lie blurted out in the heat of the moment, it's total game-over time, dude. See also **break point** and **command-Z**. A.k.a. fat lady singing, point of no return.

metabolize

To process the emotional and physical remnants of your ex until your system is rid of them, in order to go on with your life. If you have successfully completed steps 1 through 10 of the **healing process** and can indulge in **rebound sex** without needing an emergency phone session with your shrink or your mom afterward, then you have successfully metabolized your ex. Congratulations, you're ready for a new relationship! We'll be here when you get dumped again. See also **mourning period (for the dumpee)** and **mourning period (for the dumper)**.

mid-sesh smackdown

Breaking up with someone in the middle of sex, *before* they climax, as a **post-traumatic stress dis**. For example, if you discover your partner cheated on you or put a hit out on your beloved but annoying little dog, then you might stop midway through the ol' in-out, mumble "I can't do this anymore," put your clothes on, and walk out. Besides being incredibly humiliating, it increases the distance of their fall. For example, if your dumpee meets up with you when they're at level 6 on

→

the happiness scale and you break up with them, they will probably be knocked down to level 1 or 2, but if you start to have sex with them, their happiness level will rise to about 8 or 9, increasing the distance of their fall and thus their perceived pain. Trust us: you will never hear from them again. See also **fuck 'n' chuck**.

mourning period (for the dumpee)

The time it takes you to get over, or **metabolize**, the fact that you will (probably) never do the Sunday crossword, go tandem bicycling, or have oral sex with a particular person again. Assuming this person was either the love of your life or the lay of your life, give yourself at least a week to **numb the pain** by hibernating, ordering in Chinese every night, failing to wash your hair, drinking cheap wine in the afternoon, and watching a lot of romantic comedies and/or hardcore porn. Then begin the proactive portion of the **healing process**, steps 4 through 9: get in shape; help the less fortunate in order to get some perspective on your petty dating probs; get a haircut; get a piercing; buy a new iPod; have a **therapy fuck**. This period should last approximately a month. If you have any pride, avoid **second-chance sex** at all costs. If, after two months, you are confident in your personal fortitude, you may engage in **closure**. (But be warned: closure backfires more often than a Ford Pinto.) If your mourning period lasts beyond two months, consult a doctor.

THE SCENE: VERONICA (WINONA RYDER) AND J.D. (CHRISTIAN SLATER) ARE ON HIS COUCH, AND BIG FUN'S "TEENAGE SUICIDE (DON'T DO IT)" COMES ON THE RADIO. J.D. PULLS OUT A GUN AND SHOOTS THE RADIO.

VERONICA: "That's it. We're breaking up."

> [*Veronica tries to leave, but J.D. throws her back on the couch.*]

J.D.: "What? You can't bring them [*the high school classmates they've killed*] back, you must know that."

VERONICA: "I am not trying to bring anybody back, except maybe myself."

> [*J.D. kisses her, but she jumps away.*]

VERONICA: "And to think there was a time when I actually thought you were cool! Man, if you can't deal with me now, then just stay home and shoot your TV. Blow up a couple of toasters or something. Just don't come to school, and don't mess with me!"

T-CLASSIC
P SCENE OF
HERS (1989)

mourning period (for the dumper)

The time it takes you to **metabolize** someone whose heart you broke—i.e. probably, oh, two days. We're not saying you're a bad person; we're just saying that the wave of relief that comes with being the dumper (because usually you've put it off for at least a week, if not months) makes the whole thing a little easier to recover from. Sure, you might sob your heart out for twenty-four hours and wonder what the hell's wrong with you that you can't love anyone who loves you back. But the next morning, you'll spot a little honey on your morning commute and you'll bounce right back. It's a considerate gesture, however, to observe a brief, seemly mourning period after a breakup. No one likes to see their heartbreaker back on the horse within hours, so have a bit of decorum when it comes to parading around town with someone new, and consider switching to a different **online dating** service and changing your username, too. If you're sure you can be discreet, then go ahead and start slutting around town the next day. (And if you live in another state, then screw the mourning period!) But for at least a month (or longer if it was a particularly traumatic breakup), you should avoid taking a date to places where your ex or any close friends of your ex are likely to see you. Stop whining. Would it kill you to give up eating lunch at Chili's for eight weeks?

mutual decision

The unicorn of the breakup arena: a pretty little idea that doesn't actually exist in the real world, no matter how many times you insist it's true. *But wait,* you say, *what if my relationship crashed and burned in an argument that went something like this:*

→

"I hate you!"

"No, I hate *you*!"

"Fine, I'm leaving, then!"

"Good!"

"Have a nice life!"

"Don't let the door hit your ass pimples on the way out!"

How can that possibly not be mutual? you ask. Well, sure, that was a *superficially* mutual breakup, but how many relationships go from Brangelina to over in a twenty-minute argument? Your relationship has probably been building up to this screaming match for weeks, months, even years—and one of you has been hoping a little harder that it wouldn't. Chances are, after an argument like this, one of you will be just a little bit more relieved than heartbroken, and the other will be just a little bit more heartbroken than relieved.

Sure, you can go ahead and tell all your friends that the breakup was mutual—if they're good people, they won't question this fact—but if *you* know, deep down inside, that your ass was truly dumped, then don't deny yourself the full-on **healing process** and **mourning period (for the dumpee)** that you'll need. And if you know, deep down inside, that you handed *their* ass to them on a plate, then don't use that last twenty minutes as a loophole to get out of all the nice things you're supposed to do as the dumper (**see mourning period [for the dumper]**). But whatever you do, don't let on to your dumpee that you know who's the dumpee in this equation. For many mutual-decision dumpees, the belief that it was "mutual" is all that's holding them together. It's the shred of self-worth that helps them get through the night; it's the sliver of pride that gets them to the office in the morning. Taking that away from them is like stomping on kittens. (Which is why good friends never question whether the breakup was really a "mutual decision" either.) Hey, think what a terrible world this would be if nobody believed in unicorns. Fight for the magic, people. See also **endgame** for the *only* exception to this entry.

MySpace (is not our space)

❶ (*Romance-related*) The hipster messenger bag of issues that you'll have to deal with after a breakup if your couplehood was advanced enough to make itself known on your respective MySpace profiles, i.e. your "status" was marked "in a relationship," you were in each other's "top friends" lists, and you left cutesy messages in each other's comments sections.

The first dilemma you'll face is when to change your status to "single." If you're the dumper, it's a polite gesture to wait a few days before even logging in to MySpace—your dumpee will surely log in to see

if you've been online, so it's best just to make yourself scarce. Also, if you don't log in at all, your dumpee won't be left wondering, "Why did they log in and not change their relationship status? Could it be that they really love me after all?" But worse than that is if your dumpee logs in and sees that you changed your status to "single" five minutes after the breakup was officially called. As a matter of pride, you should give the dumpee the opportunity to change *their* profile to "single" first. If it's been more than a week and they still haven't updated their profile, however, then you should feel free to go ahead and change yours. However, we'd hold off on changing what you're "here for" from "friends/networking" to "dating/serious relationship" for at least a month. We're not saying that you need to hold off on actually *dating* for a whole month, but announcing it that soon on MySpace is a bit of a slap in the face.

And there are three more good reasons not to update your

MySpace profile within an unseemly matter of minutes: (a) Having patience means your ex won't "find out" via MySpace that you see this breakup as a closed case and that you won't be willing to reconsider your decision during a **closure** session (sure, they'll need to accept this at some point, but MySpace is the wrong forum). (b) Holding off also means that your ex won't suffer the humiliation of having all your mutual MySpace friends find out online first. (c) One person's breakup is another person's raging domestic argument. You might think that you're all broke up, while your partner simply thinks, "**We need to talk**." If they then log on to MySpace and see that you're suddenly "single," they've essentially been dumped on MySpace (see **public displays of affliction** [def. #2]). Harsh.

As for the comments section of your profile, however, it's okay to be a little trigger-happy with the delete button here—especially if your ex was fond of posting comments on your profile once a week, using a range of cloying pet names. Once you get back in the game, your new hookups are bound to look you up on MySpace, and no one should be subjected to their partner's snookums history. That's just too much like dirty laundry.

❷ (**Frex**-related) Sites like MySpace don't traffic much in subtleties: either you're single or you're not, either you're in someone's network or you're not, either you're "friends" or you're not. So where does that leave **frexes**? Should you keep each other in your "top friends" lists, or should you demote a frex to hanging out with your 1,247 other friends, just above Tom (the MySpace default friend that everyone gets when they sign up)? The golden rule, again, is to avoid doing anything that could be construed as a slap in the face. Don't go out of your way to demote a frex (especially if you were the dumper). But if, six months down the road, you suddenly become uber-tight with your office cubicle buddy and want

M

to promote him to your top list, just to show him how much you care, well, then we think it's okay to let a frex drift to the bottom of your list.

But what if the breakup is so acrimonious that it is clear you two will *never* be frexes? Does that person even belong on your MySpace friends list anymore? If you're in junior high and these things really *matter*, then no. Go ahead and delete them if they're really invading your personal space that much. But if you're a grown adult, can't you just let their profile sink to the bottom of your list and resolve to never click on it again? Maybe it's just us, but "deleting" an ex reeks of D & D nerdiness (with a touch of *Heathers*-esque malice thrown in). If, however, your breakup qualifies for a **post-traumatic stress dis**, then delete away. Six degrees of separation is too close for the **Fuckfaces** of this world.

❸ (*Friend-related*) **Online offing** a friend or "friend." If someone tries to weasel their way into your MySpace (or

Facebook or Friendster) inner circle, the only circumstance in which you can politely decline is if you honestly have no idea who they are—or if you've never met. It's perfectly acceptable to tell the mustachioed weirdo from your Econ 101 class that you don't feel comfortable Facebooking someone you've never spoken with. But if you *have* met the needy networker in question, then you have no choice but to accept the connection. It's not like it costs you anything to have that person in your friends list. What are you afraid of, that the captain of the cheerleading squad will stop inviting you to her parties if she finds out what losers you consort with? Netflix some old John Hughes movies to remind yourself who the cool kids *really* are. And if the friend-requester in question is evil incarnate and you would be happy never to see or hear from them again? Then simply be rude and ignore them.

If, on the other hand, you have recently **frumped** a MySpace contact with whom you once happily shared scans of your artwork, MP3s of your band, and pages of your screenplay, it's more than acceptable to let them, like frexes, fade out of your "top friends" list to mingle with the masses. But again, we'd recommend taking the higher road and only deleting them if absolutely necessary (i.e. they use your comments area to make embarrassingly desperate Wiener-Dog pleas to win your friendship back).

noncommittal breakup

An attempt to break the breakup news gently—either because you hate to see your partner hurt or because you're a big wuss, or both—that ends up feeling more like Chinese water torture, i.e. the opposite of a **Band-Aid break**. Here's the thing: When you break up with someone, you pretty much have to stand there and be the villain for an hour or two. If your dumpee is a **leg-clinger**, they're going to try and beg their way out of the breakup—or at least ask you plaintively, "Are you sure . . . ?"— and you've just got to stick to your guns. Resist the temptation to make them stop crying/ begging/throwing up by throwing them a bone. Don't display faux "uncertainty" just to soften the blow—false hope is not your dumpee's friend at this juncture. And don't weep

→

and wail about how it's the hardest decision you've ever had to make in your life and how you're so much more upset than you expected to be, blah blah blah. Okay, so a *little* of that is a nice gesture—no one wants to be dumped by a stoic, after all. But five to six hours of non-committal breakup banter is cruel and unusual punishment. Have some balls/labes and make a clean break. Tell them how hard the decision was for you to make, tell them you've thought it over and over, tell them they'll be fine without you, but always come back to "Yes, I'm sure."

At this point, a common tactic for desperate dumpees is to convince their dumper to "think things over for a week" before coming to a final decision. If you know that Osama bin Laden would tell a knock-knock joke before you'd actually reconsider your decision, then you should avoid making your dumpee spend that extra week on death row before axing them. You're basically cheating them out of a week of recovery time, not to mention forcing them to go through the same breakup *twice* (a.k.a. a **groundhog dump**). That's worse than a *Full House* rerun. And if you think they took it hard the first time, just watch how they lose the plot when you *re*-dump them and they've got no cunning wait-a-week plan to fall back on.

Finally, if your dumpee says, "If you ever change your mind, will you let me know?"—as a "friend" of ours shamelessly once did—it's okay to say yes. To insist at this point, "But I know I won't" is just plain mean—forty-eight hours later, your dumpee is already going to be groaning about what a loser they were for saying that; there's no need to make that moment of humiliation worse for them. Just be sure you don't later have a *temporary* change of heart in a weak, horny moment—unless you actually want to put their dignity through the blender. See also **overcompensation** and **goalie, playing**.

N

"not ready"

When someone says they're "not ready" for a relationship, what they really mean is, "I don't want to date *you*, loser." See also the **fortune cookie rule**.

numbing the pain

Self-destructive behavior engaged in to lessen the pain of a breakup; this is step 1 of the **healing process**. The somewhat flawed thinking goes something like this: If I cause myself pain from chain-smoking, sleeping around, getting sloppy drunk or high (to the point of passing out), and eating a lot of refined sugar, I might be distracted from the pain of this meat cleaver sticking out of my chest. After all, it's no longer important to watch my weight, eat well, or stay healthy, because life no longer matters.

While it's not the safest or sanest response, it's natural. No one expects you to be a cheery camp counselor two days after being dumped—unless you're Kelly Ripa or Tony Robbins. So go ahead and take some time out for your own personal Bridget Jones moment—get drunk on red wine in your pajamas while lip-synching "All By Myself." Rent **Shirley Valentine**, forget to shower, eat ice cream straight out of the container, get laid by that old **fuck buddy** you haven't called in a while, make a morbid **breakup mix tape** like you did in high school, etc. (This all goes for guys too, by the way . . . well, all except renting *Shirley Valentine*. Guys, you can rent porn. Actually, you girls can too!) It's been our experience that all of these activities are best conducted with a good friend (see **F.E.M.A.**) who will insist on referring to your ex as "**Fuckface**." (Well, all of these activities except the getting-laid one—unless you're into that kind of thing.)

We don't recommend numbing the pain for more than a week—two, tops. The longer the relationship, the longer you can numb, but even the end of a twenty-year marriage should not keep you literally down for more than a month or two. You *do* want to keep your job and maintain your personal hygiene habits, after all. (Trust us, you do, even though that layer of grease in your hair is kind of comforting right now.) A.k.a hitting the wall, breakdown week.

O

off-limits

The status of anyone who is seriously dating or once seri-ously dated your best friend, sibling, or parent. If your best friend/sibling/parent was dumped by this person, then the "off-limits" rule is hard and fast, for now and always. However, if the relationship was not *that* serious and your best friend/sibling/parent did the dumping, then you may, if you must, pursue them, as long as you follow the guide-lines in **going through your neighbor's trash**. On second thought, you may *not* pursue anyone your mom or dad did. That's just wrong.

on a break

The state of Ross and Rachel's relationship during season three of *Friends*. Like a pair of star-crossed lovers from

→

O

Three's Company, they decide to spend some time apart, then Ross mistakenly assumes that Rachel's starting something on the side, so Ross sleeps with Hot Xerox Girl, and when Rachel finds out, they break up for good. Well, at least until the next season, when Rachel keeps hounding him to just admit he fucked up, to which he always replies, "We were on a break!" It becomes a season catchphrase and hilarity ensues. See **break** for how and why (not) to take one.

We were on a break!

one for the road

One last shag immediately after a breakup, when the breaking-up part is officially over, but the dumper has yet to depart, i.e. you are in what is known as breakup limbo (or at least that's what you tell yourself to justify the sex). We're not naïve enough to think that we can stop people from having this kind of sex—and besides, there's nothing quite like it, if you're into that whole morbid-intense thing—but there are a few rules we must insist on: ❶ *Only* the dumpee can initiate one for the road. This rule is absolutely, unequivocally non-negotiable. ❷ The dumper should acquiesce only if he or she is reasonably sure that the dumpee can handle it and is making the move in order to leave a lasting impression, rather than to actually over-turn the decision. ❸ When a dumpee insists that they can handle it, this is not necessarily considered evidence that they

0

can. ❹ Unless the dumpee is a robot, they *will* be desperately hoping to change the dumper's mind. ❺ Even if the situation passes rules 1 through 4, the dumper should make at least one valiant attempt to resist the dumpee's come-on. ❻ If the dumpee falls for this faux demurral, the dumper should make a graceful exit, avoiding a kiss goodbye (which *will* lead to sex). Instead, the dumper should proffer a warm friendly hug (if they don't get smacked away first), say goodbye, and walk away. ❼ If rules 1 through 6 are followed to the letter and it's still game-on, the copulating couple should avoid (a) dirty talk, (b) introducing new sex acts, and (c) more than twenty minutes of post-coital pillow talk and spooning. To avoid a sunup meltdown, the dumper is advised to sleep alone tonight. A.k.a. to-go fuck. See also **sympathy fuck**.

online dating

❶ The saddle, as in, "you've got to get back in the saddle." Online dating is an ideal ego boost after being dumped, especially if you're an attractive female, but even if you're a passably attractive—or at least not so ugly that you make babies cry—male. It's also a very important aspect of step 9 of the **healing process**: going on the **rebound**. Even if you're "**just looking**" right now, nothing reminds you that you're not all alone in this world quite like logging on and scrolling through hundreds of thousands of personal ads posted by people who, just like you, are still searching for The One. See **online offing** for some handy etiquette tips for when you're ready to do more than just browse.

❷ One of the leading causes of breakups in recent years, according to our semi-professional guesstimate. Seriously, remember how much effort it used to take to cheat on your partner? You had to hang

→

out in drab hotel bars during your sales conference in Iowa, or be the sleazy employee who hits on their coworkers or assistant, or—the horror—approach strangers on your morning commute. These days, you can order up an affair from the comfort of your cubicle while enjoying the tasty and yet nutritious lunch that your sweetie brown-bagged for you—and all your coworkers will just think you're catching up on your spreadsheets. And don't even get us started on so-called monogamous parties who **Google** their old high school sweethearts "just to say hi." Here's the deal: If you're in a relationship, there's no such thing as "just looking," mmmkay?

online offing (pre-photo, pre-date)

Disconnecting from someone you became acquainted with through an **online dating** or social networking Web site, but whom you've never met

face-to-face. Hooking up via the Internet is practically virgin territory when you consider the long history of relationships. It's hard enough to know how to break up with someone your friend set you up with. Where do you begin with someone you've never even met in person?

While the Internet has brought together, across space and time, people who, less than a decade ago, would never have known each other existed, it's also—ironically—made relationships more tenuous, superficial, and fleeting. When you can't read body language, hear intonations, smell pheromones, and see people in three dimensions, how can you fully trust the connection? More often than not, you can't. Which results in a lot of online offing. It's the nature of the beast. And if you use the Internet in the hopes of getting laid/falling in love, you're going to get offed, too, no matter how cool/smart/hot/funny you are. Online dating is a numbers game—most people who get lucky online do so only after being *un*lucky with at least a handful of people. (And by "lucky," we don't just mean sex: we mean soul mate, prom date, bridge partner, whatever.)

First, let's begin with the unwelcome initiation: someone has asked to be your "friendster," "buddy," or possible "love connection." You check out their online profile and are immediately repulsed: they think that Bill O'Reilly is good for America, that Paris Hilton is a talented "artist," and that past traumas and memories have been deliberately implanted in humans by extraterrestrials to control us. How do you say "no fucking way" without saying "no fucking way"? How do you get the message across that you're thoroughly uninterested without sounding like you're rejecting a job applicant ("Thank you for your interest, unfortunately your qualifications don't meet our needs, we'll keep your resume on file")?

Emily Post would probably say that you should reply to every person who responds to your profile. She would suggest a short, polite, thanks-but-no-thanks

note—brevity is the soul of rejection, after all. Something along the lines of, "I'm flattered you wrote, but I don't think we'd be a good match." Then again, Emily Post never dated online, so what the hell did she know?

In the realm of twenty-first-century dating, whether or not you send the courtesy e-mail really depends. If the response is obviously generic ("I liked your profile, check out mine!"), then no response is necessary. Initiations from people well outside one's dating parameters do not need, let alone *deserve,* the courtesy of a response. For example, if a young woman is seeking other young women in the Minneapolis area (and her personal ad clearly states this), but some fifty-five-year-old dude from Des Moines writes in the hope of converting her (or at least getting to watch some of her Sapphic interludes), then she is within her rights to simply hit the delete button. But if the note is much more personalized and the author, who fits your parameters, clearly took some time to compose it . . . well . . . it's fine to just hit the delete button.

It sounds cruel, but that's just the way online dating works. Otherwise you might never log off. (And if you're hot, blonde, and between the ages of eighteen and twenty-five, it's going to be logistically impossible to reply personally to each and every one!) Honestly, not hearing back from someone is quite a bit more pleasant than the e-mail equivalent of having a door slammed in your face. If you *don't* hear back after replying to someone's ad, you have the liberty of assuming that they just met their true love online and forgot to hide their ad. Or maybe they suddenly lost their Internet connection in a freak home improvement–related accident. Or maybe they forgot their log-in password. Or maybe they fell into a well. It's platitudes like this that will get you through the night.

If you just don't feel right about it and want to be a better person (than us), then by all means respond, but we'd limit those responses to the ones who truly break your heart with their sincere and thoughtful pleas for your love. As gently as possible, make it clear you're not interested: "Thank you so much for the thoughtful letter; it really made my day. But I'm afraid we're just not a great match. Take good care. . . ." But consider yourself warned: Some people, especially guys, are hardwired to misinterpret signals; they remain eternal optimists in order to protect their egos. A response from you, no matter what it says, could be misread as a subconscious invitation or a test.

online offing (post-photo, pre-date)

Disconnecting from someone you became acquainted with through an **online dating** or social networking Web site and subsequently exchanged several enthused e-mails with, only to be faced later with a photo of theirs that makes your inner child cry. For this very reason, you should get the exchange of photos out of the way immediately, before any emotional bond is made via the exchange of witty repartee and cute personal anecdotes. That way, if they send you a deal-breaker—a photo with a mullet or a mole that could eat Enrique Iglesias's for breakfast—you can just drop off the face of the earth. However, we know that even after one or two e-mails, you might feel bad cutting off all contact so suddenly; it's no fun to be reminded how superficial most of us are. So here are a few of our favorite lines for dumping someone who submits an unfavorable photo. Please note: these are not the same kind of lines you may use during a face-to-face breakup or with someone you know well—those situations require a bit more delicacy. ❶ The Gentle White Lie: "I'm taking a break from online dating for a while." Warning: You may well get busted on this if you don't, in fact, take a break from online dating (or at least from that particular site) for a while. ❷ Weird Them Out—It Eases the Pain: "I can tell from the photo that you're clearly an Autumn, whereas I am a Summer—we're obviously not meant for each other." ❸ Super-Casual Truth: "Cool photo, but I'm afraid you're just not my type/I'm just not feeling this." ❹ Pay a Compliment to Cushion the Blow: "Wow, you look just like [insert hot celebrity here]. But I'm more of a [insert other hot celeb here] kind of guy/gal." ❺ Couch It in Humor: "I merged our two photos using a program called SuperGoo, and our kids turned out to be way ugly (**it's not you, it's me**)." Finally, before you engage in any knee-jerk online offing, ask yourself this: What makes you so sure you won't dig their treats? Is it possible that you're just a little too attached to your "type"? Isn't the whole point of getting online to revamp your social life? Live a little—try dating beyond your search criteria! If someone's note means enough

→

to you that you feel compelled to respond in some way, then maybe that's a sign. If the note doesn't mean a thing, then fuck 'em.

online offing (post–first date)

Disconnecting from someone you know through an **online dating** or social networking Web site, *after* you've met face-to-face. When you were mere words on the screen to one another—full of promise, endearing self-deprecation, and clever jokes—you both thought,

"How cool, we have such a great connection!" But online chemistry does not always translate into in-the-flesh chemistry. Many an online dater has fallen in love virtually, only to be crushed by the soulless reality. When you finally meet in person—hear their laugh, smell their breath, notice their funny walk, see the ring on their left hand—you may experience a desire to rush home, get online, and I.M. your virtual true love, that "other" person, about your horrible date.

How you handle Act I (i.e. the pre-date communication) can make Act II (i.e. the post-date dump) a lot less excruciating. It's all about striking a balance between knowing what you're getting into and not feeling like you owe your date anything before you've even met. While we don't recommend falling in love online, you should at least figure out if there are any major deal-breakers (e.g. they smoke, they're married with kids, they like smooth jazz). You'll also want to exchange photos (note the plural), including at least one recent one, if not a few— we've all got that one shot that fools even ourselves into thinking we should register with Barbizon. There are two schools of thought when it comes to the pre-date phone call: "it's a good idea" and "it's a crap idea." On the one hand, a little chat can confirm whether or not that quick wit really is so quick. On the other, some people just don't give good phone. Plus, then your digits are out there, like, *forever* (unless you're sneaky enough to use **disposable digits**). Either way, Act I should not be drawn out over a long period of time; meet up sooner rather than later. At least then your expectations will be fairly low, which means less disappointment if you have to "break up."

When you *do* meet up, it may take a split second to realize the reality is not measuring up to the fantasy; it may take an entire evening for it to become clear you're not a match; heck, it may take you sleeping with them to know this just isn't working out. But for simplicity's sake, we're going to assume you can tell within the first few minutes of what is essentially a blind date that you're just not that into them. While you may prefer to shake their hand and say "Hi, nice to meet you, this isn't gonna work, goodbye" with the coldness of an automated teller, that just won't do. Give them the courtesy of one drink, which is what you should limit all first dates to (at least in the planning stages). Do not excuse yourself to the bathroom never to return, do not fake an epileptic seizure, do not mention a fake STD, and do not have a friend "save" you with an "emergency call" (the oldest trick in the book). Take a deep breath and be attentive, friendly, and decidedly unflirtatious.

Finally, an eternity later, when you reach the bottom of your grande iced decaf soy mocha, it's time for the awkward goodbye. A simple "It was great to meet you" is all you need. Fight your natural instinct to make promises you can't or won't keep. If you must, just add an "I'll e-mail you" to wrap

➜

things up nicely. Of course, that means you'll *have* to follow through. But at least it's easier to let someone down gently over e-mail. In your morning-after e-dump, you can blame it on lack of chemistry—it's the truth, but it's also generic enough not to sting too badly: "Great meeting you, but I just didn't feel like we clicked. Good luck with [whatever project of theirs you discussed]. All the best. . . ." You don't have to explain it any more than that, and you don't have to stay in touch. If they preempt your closer with a request for a second date, put off any concrete planning with a "Let's e-mail tomorrow." That way it'll seem like you're not making any snap decisions. But if you've got balls or labes of steel, you can delicately lay the no-chemistry line on them right then and there.

And if it took sleeping with them on that first date to figure out this wasn't a match made in heaven? Then you must follow the rules outlined in the **face-to-face imperative** (don't worry, the entry lets you off the hook with a simple call or e-mail). For more on online offing, especially regarding long-term relationships among the tech savvy, see **MySpace** (def. #2).

over-compensation

A breakup method that involves the dumper paying the dumpee effusive, excessive compliments. In other words, **padding the fall** a little too much: "You are the most wonderful, beautiful, and caring person I've ever met" and "You are such a good soul, you deserve so much better than me" and "You are so strong and independent and powerful, you really don't need me; I just weigh you down" and "I love you so much that I can only do what's best for you, and I know you'd be better off without me" and "You are a god/dess and I am a mere mortal" and on and on and on. . . . It's an honorable attempt to boost the dumpee's self-esteem and make you, the dumper, look like an even bigger idiot in their eyes, both of which are *supposed* to ease the pain of the breakup for both parties. However, overcompensations are really just **big fat lies**, and they are particularly susceptible to attacks from dumpees who like to play **goalie**. Anyone with at least one foot on the ground will see through your obsequious flattery and resent you all the more for not giving them the courtesy of an honest (*not* brutally honest—see **cold hard truth**) breakup. But if, on the other hand, they've got their head up their ass, then be prepared to battle through a barrage of counter-arguments on why they think you are totally good enough for them. See also **noncommittal breakup**.

padding the fall

Providing your dumpee a slightly softer landing (all things being relative, of course—we don't care how many mattresses you put down, if someone's dropped from the Chrysler Building, it's still going to hurt). One of the most devastating aspects of being the dumpee is that frequently, they just don't see it coming. There they are, 723 rows into a woolly scarf they're knitting you for the impending cold snap, and out of nowhere, their sweet baby love full-body tackles them and shoves them off the ledge.

Sure, sometimes the dumpee picks up on a little "tension" between the two of you, but if they appear to be totally clueless, you've got to do a little prep work before lightening your load. The longer the relationship, the more prep

→

work necessary, of course— when dumping someone after three weeks of dating, no need to avert the surprise factor.

Basically, you just want your dumpee to feel a little in on the decision. You might withdraw, just a bit, over a day or two, for example (this is not a license to become an asshole— see **passive-aggressive breakup**). Use every ounce of willpower you have to put a moratorium on the sex. And whatever you do, don't have sex right beforehand. Begging for sexual favors at lunch can make a breakup at dinnertime that much more confusing to the dumpee. We'd even recommend a warning call simply saying "**We need to talk**"—this will give them time to mentally prepare for the worst. Otherwise, they'll think it's just another date. But make sure the call is not made more than two hours in advance; any more time to dwell on the unknown, especially if the dumpee is stuck at work, is cruel and unusual punishment.

Once the breakup is in progress, there are still ample opportunities to pad the fall. Like the '70s shrinks loved to say, put everything in "I" language ("I can't give you what you want"; "I'm not ready for marriage"; "I need to focus on my career") rather than "you" language ("You ask too much of me"; "You're so freakin' pushy"; "Would you stop calling me all the time?!"). It *is* possible to make the breakup feel at least a little mutual (see **Band-Aid break** for how), even if you know that your dumpee would jump off the Chrysler Building without a parachute if they thought it would save the relationship. Refer to past issues that the two of you never managed to resolve, so that your dumpee can begin to see this breakup as a predetermined event that neither of you had any control over. (This may also dissuade them from pursuing the dreaded "Is there **someone else**?" line of inquiry.) And say some nice things that they'll be able to cling to later, things that make them seem like the

P

catch of the century and you like the big doofus who missed the sale: emphasize what a difficult decision it was for you, what an amazing person they are, how you'd still be ordering white zinfandel with steak if it wasn't for them. But don't lay it on too thick (see **overcompensation**), or you could find yourself facing a **goalie** who will skillfully smack down every reason you have for a breakup. And no matter how many nice things you think they deserve to hear, remember to stay on target. Because forcing your dumpee to listen to three hours of breakup compliments is the equivalent of preparing a soft landing and then dangling them over the edge like Michael Jackson's baby, just so they have time to admire the view (see **noncommittal breakup**). See also **big fat lies**, **clichés**, and **cold hard truth** for more breakup speech dos and don'ts. A.k.a. cushioning the blow.

pageant sex

Ex sex initiated by the dumpee for the sole purpose of making the dumper regret their decision: "Look what you gave up, you dumbass!" As with **second-chance sex**, the initiator will show up after a **breakover** sporting an I-love-my-new-life attitude, except that with pageant sex, the initiator actually *does* love their new life. They know it's never going to work out again; they'd just like their ex to eat their heart out a little. So the sesh is more about acrobatics and less about deep eye contact than **second-chance** take-me-back sex—the intent being to impress rather than to bond. If you're the initiator,

→

you'll be on top, and you may get a little sadistic in the sack (biting, hair-pulling, name calling, facials, etc.). A.k.a. don't-you-miss-me sex, you-were-wrong-to-leave-me sex.

passive-aggressive breakup

When you're too much of a wuss to actually dump someone, so instead you act like a complete dick (that includes the ladies) until your partner is forced, as a matter of pride, to dump you. Maybe you stop inviting them along to anything you do, stop sleeping with them, and stop using your pet name for them, so they become a neurotic, insecure mess. Maybe you sleep with their roommate and "accidentally" get caught. Or maybe you just plain old stop trying. While the intention behind this is almost admirable ("I'll let them feel in control"), this is not an empowering kind of dump, so don't try that old chestnut on

us. When someone is passive-aggressively forced into a breakup like this, they don't sit at home thinking, "Thank god that pathetic excuse for a life partner is out of my life. Yay, me!" Humans just don't fall for that kind of Jedi mind trick, sorry. Either they will see through your charade and expose you as a coward, or, more likely, keep taking your crap like a punching bag, until they are a sad sack of defeat, frayed nerves, and disillusion-ment. Congratulations! In addition to leaving them all alone in this world, you've made them feel like nobody else will ever want them either.

To the uninitiated, it may seem like there is a perilously small distance between **padding the fall** and a passive-aggressive breakup. If you're having trouble telling the difference, the two rules of thumb are ❶ intent, and ❷ timing. As far as intent goes, if you're secretly hoping that your partner will get to the breakup first, then stop what-ever you're doing and have the damn **Talk** already. And as for timing: withdrawing gently over the course of a few weeks is padding the fall; letting it drag on for months while you work on updating your **online dating** profile is passive-aggressive.

passive breakup

When you're too much of a wuss to actually dump someone, so instead you hang out in the relationship for many months while waiting for an act of God to intervene, e.g. your company transfers you to Iowa, your government transfers you to Iraq, school's out, the world is ending. But unless the apocalypse is upon us, the eventual direct breakup—oh, and there will be one—will be that much more difficult and brutal. Do you really think your partner's gonna buy the fact that your sudden ability to live without them perfectly coincides with the last day of spring semester? No, they're going to know that

you've made a lame duck out of them, and they're going to make you pay for it. (If your partner isn't the vengeful type, then you'll have to dig deep and do the right thing out of an old-fashioned sense of decency instead.)

And here's another good reason to do the right thing: No matter how convinced you are that a passive breakup is just an extreme case of **padding the fall**—so much so that your partner never even knew they fell—there will be inevitable overlap with **passive-aggressive breakup** behavior. Because the longer you stick it out and the more clueless your partner remains, the more you'll start to resent them for being such a patsy. At first you'll pity them, then you'll start to find them pathetic, and then plain annoying, at which point it will be impossible to treat them with the little tenderness that they deserve.

The only excuse for hesitation is if your partner has an imminent life-changing exam or job interview—the bar exam

→

counts, but their weekly trivia night does not. And "imminent" means weeks, not months. Plus, don't postpone a breakup just because it's almost Valentine's Day or their birthday or the holidays (see **crappy holidays**)—that's condescending and totally counterproductive. (Seriously, how much do they *not* want that Vermont Teddy Bear that you bought out of a sense of duty two days before putting their heart, not to mention all those warm fuzzy feelings, through the blender?) See **rent control** and **unilateral dump**.

pet dump

❶ Trying to get your partner to break up with their own pet, because it exacerbates your allergies, shits on (or in) your new shoes, attacks you whenever you come near your partner, humps your leg, takes up half the bed at night, and/or creepily stares at you while you have sex. You may see your partner's pet as a bad habit you wish they would quit, like smoking or biting their toenails. But serious animal lovers (i.e. the kind who have mini outfits custom-made for their pets to match their own, or who treat their pets to massage therapy . . . or just plain therapy) think of their pets as their own offspring. So if you're going to ask your partner to choose between you and the dog, then you should be fully prepared for them to pick the dog. Which leads us to def. #2 . . .

❷ Breaking up with your partner because they love their pet more than you.

MOVIE BREAKU
MOST RESEMB
DEODORANT C
BRIDGET JONI

THE SCENE: BRIDGET JONES [RENÉE ZELLWEGER] QUITS HER JOB BECAUSE AN
AFFAIR WITH HER SLEAZY BOSS [HUGH GRANT] WENT AWRY, AND WHEN HER
BOSS OFFERS HER A PROMOTION TO GET HER TO STAY, SHE REPLIES:

> "Thank you, Daniel, that is very good to
> know. But if staying here means working
> within ten yards of you, frankly, I'd rather
> have a job wiping Saddam Hussein's arse."
>
> [*Cue Aretha Franklin's "Respect" as she
> walks out.*]

P SCENE THAT
ES A GO-GIRL
MMERCIAL:
S'S DIARY (2001)

post-traumatic stress dis

A breakup, resulting from a partner's betrayal, that's intended to return some of the pain they caused. Everyone deserves to be dumped humanely, with dignity and respect—unless, of course, they stole your credit card and racked up massive debt, told your boss you still wet the bed, cheated on you, cheated on you with your best friend, cheated on you with one of your parents, etc. If any of these are the case, then the rules outlined in "How to Break Up with Someone (in Thirteen-and-a-Half Easy Steps)" (page 10) do not apply. You can forgo the **face-to-face imperative** and forget the niceties.

Extreme forms of P.T.S.D. operate under the "two wrongs make a right" philosophy. This includes reporting them to the I.R.S./police/Homeland Security for real or imagined misdeeds, posting humiliating (possibly naked) photos of them on the Web, performing a **mid-sesh smackdown**, writing a tell-all memoir that goes into great detail about their sexual short-comings, and, of course, fucking *their* best friend/parent. In other words: sweet, sweet **revenge**. But be warned: This is playing with karmic fire, and if you do not act with all your facts straight or with reasonable restraint, you could get burned . . . again (especially if they're in possession of incriminating nude photos of *you*).

We recommend more conscientious P.T.S.D.s. You could certainly confront them with a laundry list of their physical flaws and idiot moments, but realize they may retaliate with their own list of your flaws, simply as a defense mechanism—then you'll be subjected to *double* the indignity. Why not keep it short and bittersweet: "Thanks for destroying my faith in humanity. If I ever see you again, it'll be too soon." Or simply cut your partner off cold: nothing as dramatic as the silent treatment, just zero emotional response, total blank civility. But be sure they know why you're leaving, so they can

➜

P

perhaps learn from their mistakes and not torture another innocent sucker. Then leave immediately. It may not give you the same immediate satisfaction of a confrontation on *Jerry Springer,* but you'll be able to live with yourself for years to come (and you won't have to worry about Homeland Security coming after your ass for wasting their time).

preemptive breakup

When you have to break up with someone who's really into you even though no relationship really exists between you, just so they stop living in a fantasy world. Perhaps you're office lunch buddies, but you keep catching them making moony eyes at you over the cubicle dividers, or you're next-door neighbors and they keep popping over to borrow a cup of sugar . . . at 11:00 P.M . . . and insist on repaying you with a bottle of wine . . . and their company.

If they haven't explicitly conveyed their intentions and you don't want to seem presumptuous, then we suggest you start by dropping hints— big, dense, two-ton hints—about other people you are interested in romantically, about things going on with your partner (real or imagined), about how refreshing it is to have a platonic guy/girl friend to talk to about this stuff, etc. This *should* work. In a rational world where hormones don't cloud our logic and good sense, this *would* work. But damn it, we don't live in that kind of world. They may misconstrue the conversations about your romantic life as sure signs of your romantic interest in *them.* Hell, if they're really whipped, they could interpret the way your left elbow points toward them when you fold your arms while sitting at your desk as hard evidence of your undying love and lust for them. (Hope is a thing with feathers and no brain.)

If you suspect that your storytelling hasn't put them off, then it's time for **the Talk**.

You know: "I never mix business with pleasure," "**It's not you, it's me**," "I really care about you as a *friend*," "I really value our friendship and don't want to jeopardize it" . . . (Insert platitude here; see **clichés** for more suggestions.) If you fear you're leading them on, then in their eyes you probably are, so just lay down the law. Be a rock, be an island. A.k.a. didn't you get the memo? Not to be confused with the highly unnecessary **premature evacuation**.

premature evacuation

When someone tries to have a serious, sit-down **Talk** with you before it's really necessary or appropriate, like after a first date, or over e-mail before a blind date. Premature evacuation often afflicts those with an inflated sense of self, a tenuous grasp on reality, and a summer home on Planet Areyoufuckingkiddingme. Those predisposed to it are often guilty of unnecessary full disclosures, too.

Not to be confused with the highly *necessary* **preemptive breakup**.

public displays of affliction (P.D.A.)

❶ Breakups that occur within earshot of innocent bystanders. Frequently an unintended— though thoroughly deserved— consequence of **pulling a librarian** (the cowardly act of breaking up with someone in a place where outbursts are frowned upon).

Locations where P.D.A. are acceptable (i.e. where gawking onlookers are more likely to be entertained than inconvenienced by the scene): dive bars, fast-food joints, sidewalks, public parks, keggers, and supermarket checkout lines. Locations where P.D.A. are to be avoided at all costs: public transportation, your cubicle (on the phone or in person), the gym, birthday parties or weddings, romantic restaurants,

➜

actual libraries, and long lines at Disneyland. See also **chopping block**.

❷ When breakups are announced in the public domain *before* the decision has been made known to the dumpee, e.g. posting it to your blog, updating your **MySpace** profile to read "status: single," leaving a message on an answering machine they share with roommates, announcing it on Oprah's talk show (cf. Matt Damon and Minnie Driver, circa 1998), reposting your **online dating** ad, e-mailing everyone in your address book to ask for help moving out of the apartment you share, asking someone else to prom.

R

rebound, on the

A period of deliberate, self-imposed romantic and/or sexual distraction intended to help in the post-breakup **healing process**. If you're a recent dumpee (or, perhaps, a dumper), you may hope to accomplish one or more of the following by going on said rebound: ❶ Prove to yourself that you're *so* over your ex. ❷ Remind yourself that you're not all alone in this world. ❸ Remind yourself that you're not yet past your sell-by date. ❹ Distract yourself from the cavernous well of grief and loneliness festering inside you (see **therapy fuck**).

There are many ways to engage in rebound behavior: update your **online dating** profile (it's okay to just hang out on there and enjoy the attention for a bit), engage in **flirting therapy** (it's okay to be "**just looking**" right now), hit the town looking fabulous (pick a

R

designated dialer in case you fall prey to the **drunken dialies**), **masturbate** chronically (who says you can't be your own rebound?). If you decide that you're ready for **rebound sex**, steer clear of **fucksimiles**. And whatever you do, keep things light and airy for now—no **impulse buys**! If you're afraid you may succumb, then you might want to consider a temporary bout of **celibacy** instead. In fact, do not attempt to get back in the game too soon after a split; ideally, you should wait until you've accomplished steps 1 through 8 of the **healing process** in some capacity before going on the rebound. That said, sometimes a quick **therapy fuck** is all you need to get back on your feet.

rebound sex

Post-breakup casual relations, most commonly in the form of a one-night stand. "Rebound sex" is an umbrella term for the various forms of fleeting coitus that take place after a breakup

and before you're ready for a full-on relationship–in other words, sex will always be preceded by some kind of adjective until you've moved on. Along with the intended benefits of going on the **rebound**, you may also hope to accomplish one or more of the following with a quick roll in the hay: ❶ Prove to yourself that your ex wasn't *all that* in bed. ❷ Close your eyes and pretend you're with **Fuckface** (see **fucksimile**). ❸ Distract yourself, however briefly, from the gaping chest wound of your breakup (see **therapy fuck**). ❹ Cleanse your palate for your next serious relationship (see **sorbet**). ❺ "Break the seal" on your inability to even consider sex with someone besides your ex, i.e. you figure that if you just get the damn thing over with already, no matter how bad it is, the next time will feel a little more natural, and maybe even good. ❻ Test the waters to see if you're "ready" to be out there, which may prevent you from the humiliation of agreeing to a blind date and spending

➜

the entire evening sobbing about how heartbroken you still are (it's hard to sob if you're drunk and fucking, though it has been known to happen—if you think you may be at risk, we recommend not sleeping over). ❼ Achieve orgasm.

Rebound sex tends to be a cheerier affair after fairly mild breakups (i.e. when you *weren't* deeply in love), because the temporary transfer of affections is uplifting ("Look how easy it is to get another crush!") rather than depressing ("I can't believe I have to go back to all this shallow bullshit!"). Generally speaking, rebound sex feels nicer in your twenties than it does in your thirties— for the latter demographic, **masturbation** is often the preferable option. But for all participants, there is the risk that rebound sex will feel kind of like eating the entire tub of ice cream: pretty damn good at the time (and with every spoonful, you'll be thinking, *I deserve this*), but an hour later you'll be feeling a little sick (and, most likely, thinking, *I deserve this*).

Rejection Hotline

One of the twenty-first century's greatest inventions: local telephone numbers in just about every major American city that, when called, play a recorded message explaining that the person who gave you this number did not want you to have their real digits for any number of reasons (you're not their type, you have bad breath, you give off that creepy psycho stalker vibe, or you seem "as appealing as playing leapfrog with unicorns"—that's a direct quote!). RejectionHotline.com, the Web site, argues that this is a genuine public service: "The rejector has an easy way to get rid of unwanted suitors, to express a lack of interest in a non-confrontational manner, and to gracefully escape an uncomfortable situation. The rejectee, on the other hand, is able to hear the bad news in the privacy of his/her own home without being subjected to the embarrassment and/or

R

ridicule of a more public rejection. Furthermore, there are no unanswered 'what-ifs,' no desperate assumptions of 'I must have just misdialed,' and no ambiguity—all of which are common by-products of the randomly selected fake numbers that were more common before the advent of the Rejection Hotline." See also **Dear John dot coms**.

rent control

When an unfriendly real estate market affects the schedule or structure of your breakup— perhaps you break up but continue living together, the dumper on the couch, until one of you finds a new place (*hello,* **ex sex** and messy fallout!), or you postpone initiating a breakup until your lease comes up for renewal, and then use the letter from your landlord as a natural segue into **the Talk**. Rent control is most common among the young and broke, and in cities where rents are sky-high and the perfect apartment is even harder to come by than the perfect boyfriend or girlfriend. If the decision is mutual and entirely unavoidable—i.e. you agree to temporarily bunk together because neither of you has a friend with a futon—then who are we to tell you to waste a whole month's paycheck on a sublet just to achieve more perfect "**closure**"? But beware of unilaterally giving in to rent control, e.g. timing your dump speech so you don't have to break your lease and lose your security deposit. As we outlined in **passive breakup**, few dumpees will fail to notice your perfect timing, and nothing turns the knife like making them feel less important than

→

R

a month's rent. See also *The Break-Up* (2006), starring Jennifer Aniston and Vince Vaughn, also starring the perfect Chicago condo that neither of them is willing to sacrifice.

retail therapy

Shopping as a breakup recovery tool. Why should you spend money on yourself after a dump? Because you're worth it! Or at least to make yourself feel like you're worth something; buying shit you don't need may give you a sense of worth, a sense of entitlement, a sense of well-being. (For that you can thank our crass corporate culture . . . and Apple for making all their new gadgets so shiny and pretty.) Sure, that warm fuzzy feeling is false and fleeting, but so is the hope that you'll learn from your mistakes and never be hurt again—both illusions help move the recovery process along. And when you can't have what you want in a partner, there's some comfort in having what you want in a new jacket or a new cell phone. (And if these items are well-made, they'll be more reliable than your ex.) Retail therapy is most effective when practiced as part of a breakup makeover, or **breakover**, rather than simply as a way to fill the void inside of you. For instance, fifteen pairs of new shoes won't make **Fuckface** come crawling back, but splurging on a pair of high-end running shoes to inspire you to get out of the house, go to the gym, work out your rage, and get in great shape may help you move on. Give yourself a week to blow your budget; you can catch up on bills next month. But limit yourself to a week: no **impulse buys** or Mike Tyson-esque shopping sprees on pet tigers.

R

BEST MOVIE B
THAT BREAKS
WALL: THE LO

LARRY HUBBARD (STEVE MARTIN) COMES HOME TO FIND HIS GIRLFRIEND IN
BED WITH ANOTHER GUY. IT'S A MURPHY BED, SO HE JUST FLIPS IT CLOSED,
THEN TURNS TO THE CAMERA WITH A RATHER CRAZED LOOK ON HIS FACE
AND SAYS,

"I think I handled that rather well."

LATER HE GOES UP TO THE ROOF TO CALL OUT HIS BELOVED'S NAME.
THERE ARE GUYS ON ALL THE OTHER ROOFS CALLING OUT THEIR BELOVEDS'
NAMES TOO:

"DANIELLE! I LOVE YOU!"

EAKUP SCENE THE FOURTH NELY GUY (1984)

returner's remorse

The regret felt after dumping someone, i.e. "Oh god, what have I done?" often as a result of witnessing the results of your dumpee's **breakover**. Plus, once your ex is back on the shelf, they suddenly don't seem so bad anymore. The newer models are all bells and whistles, no real substance. And what used to drive you crazy about your ex is now sweet and endearing: the way they ate with gusto (i.e. their mouth open), the way they encouraged (nagged) you to get a better job, the way their infectious (grating) laugh made you feel warm and safe. It's a classic case of wanting what you can't have and not wanting what you *do* have. And though Hollywood abuses this kind of remorse as a plot device in romantic comedies to allow the protagonist to overcome their own internal obstacles, find redemption, and live happily ever after with the dumpee, it rarely works out like that in the real world. Changing your mind because you're feeling a little nostalgic and horny usually results in pathetic groveling; if the dumpee takes you back, it's usually only a matter of days (hours, even) before you start suffering **buyer's remorse**, after which you'll end up putting them through the hell of a breakup all over again (see **groundhog dump**).

returning to the well

❶ **Ex sex**. ❷ Getting back together with your ex. Often the beginning of **eternal return**.

revenge

The act of publicly humiliating someone after they dump you, e.g. calling in to your ex's local radio show and sending out an I-love-you-so-much-it-hurts dedication to her boyfriend of one week on her behalf; handing out flyers in your ex's

→

neighborhood that advertise him as a cheating scumbag, à la Samantha on *Sex and the City*; e-mailing your pet name for your ex to all his coworkers; creating a fake **MySpace** profile for your ex (if she's not on the site already) and making her look like a no-friends loser ("Hero: Kelly Ripa—she's just so thin and perky!!"); blogging about your **revenge fuck**. Unfortunately for you, however, the world is full of high-road types who don't look kindly on such tactics— these folks are likely to gossip all over town about what a small-minded, low-road ho you are. *Now* who's humiliated, sucker? For the kind of revenge that leaves you untouchable, go for a **breakover** instead.

revenge fuck

Sleeping with your ex's nemesis, roommate, sibling, parent, or pet in order to pay them back for dumping you. In one sense, it totally works: how could your ex *not* be grossed out/horrified/disillusioned/ damaged for life? But unless your ex is a few peas short of a casserole, your cunning plan is sure to backfire, because they'll know exactly why you slept with their paste-eating dork of a sibling, and the most overwhelming emotion they will feel is deep, abiding pity for you. And we're not talking about the kind of pity that leads to a **sympathy fuck**, either. We mean the kind of pity that makes someone look away in secondhand embarrassment. Feel better now? See also **hate fucking**.

reverse dump

The breakup equivalent of "You can't fire me because I quit!" It's a desperate yet understandable attempt to save face and regain some control during a process that is wholly embarrassing and emotionally destabilizing. While it would never hold up in a court of love, the comfort it can give the original dumpee cannot be underestimated: the reverse dumper may be living on Fantasy Island, but at least there they get to be smart, beautiful, and single by choice. Unscientific studies have shown that those who engage in reverse dumps experience greater job satisfaction and more regular orgasms compared with **leg-clingers**. A.k.a. boomerang breakup.

rhetorical breakup

Using a question to segue into **the Talk**, e.g. "Do you think we should go out anymore?" or "Do you think things are working out between us?" or "Do you think we're really making each other happy?" If you've done a good job of **padding the fall**,

this line of conversation may make your potential dumpee feel like part of the decision-making process. But if this is a **stealth dump**, then you may as well tell your partner that you'd rather date someone more attractive (perhaps someone whose eyes aren't set so close together)— because a question like one of the above, out of the blue, will sting just as much.

rock bottom

The post-breakup low point when you know that things can only . . . *must* only get better from here. For example, audibly weeping in the personal lubricant aisle at CVS; walking twenty blocks in the rain to call your ex from a pay phone so you can hear them say "Hello" before hanging up because you can't remember how to do *72; resorting to peeing in a jar, Howard Hughes–style, just to be sure you don't miss your ex calling when your phone is charging in the living room and you're in the can. It is at these

→

moments when you catch a glimpse of yourself in a mirror or realize what you must look like to passersby, and your lazy survival instinct finally gets up off its ass and shakes some sense into you. As the inspirational music swells in the background (see **I will survive**), you dry your eyes, wash your hair, empty your piss jar, and get back in the saddle of life.

rose-colored hindsight

Idealizing your recent relationship, which usually includes playing that montage of fond memories over and over in the theater of your mind with the Dolby surround-sound system playing Muse or Maroon 5 on repeat. Avoiding this sort of behavior is step 3 of the **healing process**. If you're the dumper, you may suffer the opposite of **buyer's remorse**: **returner's remorse**. If you're the dumpee, resist the temptation to put on those rose-colored glasses. No good can come of it; you'll simply end up feeling *more* inadequate, lonely, and depressed. Instead, focus on **Fuckface**'s faults. There must be at least one (besides their ability to live without you), even if it's just a malformed pinkie toe or a tendency to douse every meal in ketchup. However, we're guessing that Fuckface is afflicted by one, if not all, of the following: selfishness, insensitivity, immaturity, hypocrisy, a tendency to be vanilla in bed (take your pick!). And remind yourself how few faults you have in comparison. You're practically perfect!

R

S

saving Silverman

When your friends attempt a mid-relationship cock block because they think that a clean slate is just what you need, even if you don't know it yet (their justification is that you're too damn wimpy/clueless/whipped to initiate the necessary breakup yourself). From the 2001 movie of the same name, in which Jack Black and Steve Zahn kidnap their buddy's high-maintenance, domineering girlfriend and then set him up with his old high school sweetheart to try and make him forget that he was about to propose. Less extreme tactics for saving Silverman include:

❶ Dragging your buddy along to boys'/girls' night, getting them shitfaced, and convincing them that "what Pookie doesn't know won't hurt Pookie." Then telling on them. ❷ Not including your friend's partner in any social plans, or not paying any attention to them when they do show up. ❸ Using subtle "negs" to convey your opinions to your friend: "Wow, your new fling's got a great personality," "it's really neat how you go for inner beauty," etc. ❹ Luring your friend's partner into a drunken make-out sesh and then telling on them.

People, monogamy is a sometimes fragile thing that can use all the nurturing it can get. Such "friends" as these risk a karmic **post-traumatic stress dis** that will leave them reeling for years. Sure, everyone hates to see their buddy with the wrong person, and if you're really convinced they're making a dire mistake, then you can attempt to tell them this, *kindly*. But be prepared for a seriously diminished friendship with this person if they go on to marry that big fat loser anyway.

say my name

A frequently cited factor in breakups: when your partner gets your name wrong, particularly when it happens mid-coitus. However, not all misnomers are deserving of a dump. For example, if your boyfriend of two months accidentally refers to you as Katie instead of Katy in an e-mail, we think you could probably let it slide—it clearly isn't one of those does-he-really-love-me issues, and it's a hundred times more benign than forgetting your birthday or calling out someone else's name during sex (neither of which are necessarily deal-breakers either, for

the record). It's not even as bad as leaving a wad of hair in the bathtub. It's all about context. For example, "Katie" beats out "Katy" on Google by 12.5 million to 3.4 mil, and Katie Couric is, like, *everywhere.* Sure, if this happened on a regular basis, you'd be right to be bummed— *ongoing* carelessness is something to be concerned about. But one-off fuck-ups as a result of multitasking? We think you should let it go. One time a lovelorn reader, seeking advice, began an e-mail to us with "Dear Abby." But she apologized profusely in a follow-up e-mail, and we got over it—we even answered her question. We've all had those relationship moments: "He forgot how many Splendas I take in my soy mocha latte?!" or "I can't believe she didn't remember to TiVo *The Daily Show* for me!" or "He *knows* that baby carrots creep me out." Something like this happens after a bad day at the office, and it can make you feel like your whole relationship is a sham. It's not, you know—

→

or, at least, this isn't a symptom of a sham. Hey, just be glad that your name is spelled the cool way—'cause you know that most of the Katies out there dot their "i" with a little heart. Now *there's* a deal-breaker.

But what if your partner *does* scream out someone else's name right as they come (a.k.a. bedroom bloopers)? And what if that name is their ex, or their hot coworker, or their sibling? Okay, so the sibling thing is beyond the scope of this book, but are you *really* going to dump someone because they accidentally used a name that they called out twice a day for two years? We know it's unpleasant to think about, but we don't get to dump our partners just because they used to sleep with other people and that makes us feel funny. And as for that hot coworker: so your partner's mind wandered during sex. It's a huge bummer, to be sure, but is it *really* a dumpable offense? Again, it's all about context, and the only way to get that is to talk about

it. *Calmly*. Remember, your partner didn't magically stop being attracted to other people the moment they met you, and if you're looking for someone who will be faithful to you in their every single thought, then we sure hope you like cats. Maybe your partner was just fantasizing about a hot three-way with you and the coworker—which is about a zillion times better than them cheating on you with that hot coworker, dontcha think? Or maybe their mind wandered because their hot coworker happened to wear really tight pants that day (we bet V.P.L. has been responsible for more than a handful of such solecisms). It's okay to be bummed about this, and if it happens on a regular basis, then you're right to be suspicious—but one mid-booty brain fart does not a lyin' cheatin' asshole make. See also **Chicken Little syndrome**.

second-chance sex

Ex sex initiated by the dumpee for the sole purpose of reconciliation. The initiator will get their ex to agree to a meeting under the false pretense of the dumpee needing **closure**. Of course, said dumpee will show up in a new outfit, with a new gym body, and fronting an I-love-my-new-life attitude. During the closure conversation, the dumpee will appear to accept and understand all of the dumper's explanations for the breakup. And then, as the closure is coming to a close, they will oh-so-casually suggest a drink at the local bar "for old times' sake." Which leads to another, which leads to . . . *exactly*. The sex will be intense and fantastic, but their heart will break all over again when their partner reaches for a condom and sheepishly refers to his or her "recent activity." In the entire history of breakups and closure, second-chance sex has worked exactly twice. Every other time it ends in tears—a **groundhog dump**. Don't do it, Petal, or you'll never be able to sing Human League's "Don't You Want Me" at karaoke again without losing your shit. A.k.a. take-me-back sex, pathetic.

sex toys

Invaluable tools to help you conquer the **masturbation** portion of step 9 of the **healing process**. For help in deciding how to arm yourself, check out our companion manual *Sex Toy: An A–Z Guide to Bedside Accessories*.

S

sexual reorientation

The desire, announcement to your best friend, or actual attempt to abandon your current sexual orientation for another in the hopes of avoiding the kind of nuclear breakup you just experienced, typically during step 1 of the **healing process**. It's a phenomenon most often seen among straight women (and a few as-yet-undiscovered lesbians) who've just been cheated on by a male partner with one or more of the following character flaws: he's controlling, jealous, macho, stupid, manipulative, alcoholic, unemployed, and/or obsessed with sports (to the point where his idea of romance is getting a blow job during half-time). A woman's utter disappointment in and disgust with her ex-boyfriend/husband is projected onto all male members of the human race, resulting in a profound though usually fleeting disinterest in heterosexual sex, which, with her ex, was often just ten minutes of orgasmless (for her) jackhammering. When faced with the prospect of a long, lonely life without companionship or cuddling, she turns her attention to the female of the species, recalling fondly those delightful tickle fights she had with her best friend in elementary school, remembering how she thought the girl-on-girl action in *Bound* and on *The O.C.* was kind of hot, and thinking how easy and effortless it is to talk with her current girl friends, how they'll listen to and empathize with her problems instead of trying to solve them. What could be better than getting your nails done *with* your partner? Who wouldn't want to date someone who could understand the throes of PMS, loan you a great hand-embroidered clutch, and kiss you without jamming their tongue down your throat?

Of course, it's a nice little fantasy. But as any lesbian will tell you: Like math, relationships are hard, no matter what your sexual orientation. And all creatures are not created

→

equally. There are plenty of decent guys who hate sports, love opera, and are not gay. Just as there are plenty (okay, several) lesbians who are controlling, jealous, macho, stupid, manipulative, alcoholic, unemployed, and/or obsessed with sports. If a post-breakup sexual reorientation gives you comfort, encourages a bout of rejuvenating **celibacy**, lets you experiment sexually, or perhaps helps you discover your true sexual identity, more power to you! Just be sure you keep your expectations realistic: high ones (the kind your partner probably couldn't measure up to) are what helped get you here in the first place.

doorman tell the person you're seeing that you've moved when they stop by to say hi. The name of this activity alone should be enough to shame you out of doing it. See also **Dear John dot coms**.

S

Shannen, pulling a

Having a friend or acquaintance break up with someone on your behalf, named for the TV show *Breaking Up with Shannen Doherty* (one in a long line of Doherty train wrecks). For example, you have your

Shirley Valentine

Rx rental for a woman who has been recently dumped. Take one viewing with a bottle of Two-Buck Chuck and a good **F.E.M.A.**; call your mom (*not* your ex) in the morning.

[ANSWERING MACHINE]: "Hi, this is Nikki [BROOKE LANGTON].
Leave a message."

MIKE [JON FAVREAU]: "Hi. Uh, Nikki, this is Mike. I met you at
the, um, at the Dresden, uh, tonight. Uh, I just
called to say that I had a great time, and you
should call me tomorrow, or in, uh, two days,
uh, whatever. Anyway, uh, my number is. . ."
[answering machine cuts him off]

[ANSWERING MACHINE]: "Hi, this is Nikki. Leave a message."

MIKE: "Hi, uh, Nikki, this is Mike again. I just called
'cause it sounded like your machine
might've cut me off when, uh, when I, before
I finished leaving my number. Anyway, uh,
and also, uh, sorry to call so late, but you
were still at the Dresden when I left, so I

knew I'd get your machine. Anyhow, uh, uh, my number's. . ."
[*answering machine cuts him off*]

[ANSWERING MACHINE]: "Hi, this is Nikki. Leave a message."

MIKE: "That's it. Just wanna leave my number. I didn't want you to think I was weird or desperate or, we should just, uh, hang out and, uh, see where it goes. 'Cause it's nice and, uh, you know, no expectations. So, okay? Thanks a lot. Bye-bye."

[ANSWERING MACHINE]: "Hi, this is Nikki. Leave a message."

MIKE: "I just got out of a six-year relationship, okay? That should help explain why I'm acting so weird. I just wanted you to know that. It's not you, it's me. I'm sorry. This is Mike."

➜

[ANSWERING MACHINE]: "Hi, this is Nikki. Leave a message."

MIKE: "Hi, Nikki, this is Mike. Could you just, uh, call me when you get in? I'm gonna be up for a while and I'd rather speak to you in person instead of trying to fit it all into. . ." [*answering machine cuts him off*]

[ANSWERING MACHINE]: "Hi, this is Nikki. Leave a message."

MIKE: "Uh, Nikki? Mike. It's, uh, uh, it's just, uh, this just isn't working out. I think you're great, but, uh, I, maybe we should just take some time off from each other. It's not you, it's me. It's what I'm going through. All right? Uh, it's only been six months. . . ."

NIKKI: "Mike?"

MIKE: "Nikki! Great! Did you just walk in, or were you listening all along?"

NIKKI: "Don't ever call me again."

someone else

Sadly, one of the most common reasons for breakups. You're feeling restless, underappreciated, stifled, and bored in your current, theoretically monogamous, relationship when fate (or Craigslist) suddenly introduces you to someone who makes you feel alive, who understands your point of view, who doesn't yet know or care about all your many flaws, and who will happily engage in strap-on sex (unlike *some* people). Should you decide to enter into a secret affair, with no intention of fessing up to partner A (or even partner B, perhaps), you run the risk of being found out, to say nothing of the bad karma, bad luck, and bad vibes such bad behavior will automatically attract. If—and usually it's just a question of when—you *are* found out, brace yourself for a **post-traumatic stress dis** of the highest order, which will probably involve serious **collateral damage**. You may even end up with a **bunny-boiler** on your hands. All good reasons to

keep it in your pants and either try couples counseling or else end it.

If you *do* decide to end your relationship rather than waiting around to get busted (or, better yet, you decide to end your relationship before going "all the way" with your piece on the side), then you've got to be prepared for the big breakup question: "Is there someone else?" As a general rule, don't tell them anything they don't really need to know. It may feel good to get the truth off your chest, but your comfort should not be your priority here—after all, you've got someone waiting in the wings to comfort you with hugs and oral sex; all your partner has is a tub of gelato. So no blurting out "I slept with Casey from Accounting last night," or, worse, "I slept with Casey from Accounting last night, and I think I'm in love." Even better if you didn't actually sleep with Casey yet (and for the record, deciding that you're *on the verge* of breaking up doesn't make sleeping with Casey cool—see **unilateral**

→

S

dump). If you've already done the dirty with "someone else" (shame on you), then only mention this if (a) this someone else is a friend of theirs (otherwise you both are making a fool of your original partner), or (b) you may have compromised your original partner's sexual health (if you slept with partner B and then again with partner A, you very well may have). Otherwise, zip it. In theory, partner A wants to know; in practice, they don't. A.k.a. third-party rules.

sorbet

A post-breakup, palate-cleansing lay to help prepare yourself for a new long-term relationship. For example, perhaps you're worried that the first time you sleep with someone other than **Fuckface**, you're going to start weeping right as you come— so why not get this moment over with on a one-night stand that doesn't mean anything to you? Or maybe you could use

an uncomplicated orgasm to remind you that your ex isn't the exclusive leaseholder on your sexual pleasure. More extended sorbets may take the form of a brief fling. This is particularly common after a sexless relationship that left you feeling unsatisfied, unattractive, and unwanted. A month of no-strings-attached sex— because, let's face it, many women simply can't get off on a one-night stand—can be like sexual rehab, leaving you feeling sexed up, hotter than Georgia asphalt, and more sought after than a tub of lube at a circle jerk. In other words, relationship-ready!

splitting assets

Deciding who gets what restaurants, bars, friends, books, CDs, etc. post-breakup. As with alimony, you should make a distinction between favorites that were acquired *during* the relationship, and those that were preexisting conditions. What was yours before the relationship remains yours after the relationship—same goes for your ex. But as for items, people, book clubs, pets, and dining preferences acquired as a couple—the person being dumped gets first dibs on everything, be it a favorite park bench or the cat. (Note: For books and CDs, "first dibs" doesn't mean the dumpee gets to keep everything. Rather, they get to divide the property into two piles—"She never fully appreciated Carly Simon anyway," etc. As long as the piles are close to even, the dumper doesn't get to dispute the split.) If you both had the same local watering hole before you started dating (maybe that's where you met) or you had a mutual friend (maybe that's who introduced you), then the person being dumped gets first dibs on that, too. Certain extenuating circumstances may apply, however—for example, if the dumper's twin brother manages the bar in question, or the mutual friend is the dumper's primary confidant and just a work acquaintance

of the dumpee, or the dumpee is in the habit of kicking the cat. But as a general rule, the one whose heart has been put through the blender claims the social detritus of the relationship. And as for that mythical unicorn, the **mutual decision** breakup? You freaks of nature clearly don't need our help— we're sure you're fully capable of discussing each issue maturely, like the evolved beings you obviously are, and coming to an acceptable, er . . . what's that word again? Oh yeah: *compromise.*

spring cleaning

❶ The preponderance of breakups right as the weather turns nice and spring fever starts to trump that comfy old long-term relationship that comforted you through the long winter like a pair of well-worn wool socks. **❷ Cutting the cord**.

STD scare

❶ The natural, knee-jerk inclination to dump someone after they admit, *before* you sleep together, to having an STD. One of the biggest problems with STDs is the stigma attached to them—which is almost irrational when you consider how incredibly common they are: the majority of sexually active people will have an STD at some point in their lives. It *seems* like it's a lot fewer than that because people still don't talk about STDs openly and honestly. And they don't talk about them openly and honestly because people still like to assume—incorrectly—that only promiscuous lowlifes get STDs. Which means that the few brave souls who *do* fess up are forced to take one for the team and risk getting prematurely dumped.

Instead, you should give them a medal for leading the way on the path of safer-sex righteousness. Everyone needs to get used to having the tough conversations—the more often they occur, the easier they get. Asking questions of the people you're having sex with (or better yet, *planning* on having sex with) and answering your partners' questions with good information and without attitude

S

→

("Do I *look* like a promiscuous lowlife to you?!") should be a given. And with a little well-researched information from reliable health resources like PlannedParenthood.org and AshaSTD.org, there'd be a whole lot fewer knee-jerk "no" reactions.

Besides, what makes you so sure *you* don't have any STDs? Some infections are difficult to test for, especially if you're a guy, and especially if you're not showing any symptoms—and a ton of people are carriers of STDs, like herpes, without *ever* showing symptoms! Plus, doctors won't always test for all STDs, even when you ask for the whole nine yards. You have to ask explicitly for the test for each STD. And then of course, there's the incubation period—the time it takes for a disease to show up on results. Finally, though condoms are an excellent way to reduce risk, they don't always protect you from everything. All this is to say that it's hard to be 100 percent sure, just like it's almost impossible to be 100 percent

safe. That doesn't mean you shouldn't try to keep yourself educated about your sexual health status at all times, or that you shouldn't use barrier protection or birth control every time. Sex is messy and can be dangerous—it's the nature of the beast with two backs.

So if someone you're dating says they have or once had something, take a big breath and think twice about running for the door. It takes a lot of courage for someone to open up about their sexual health, and though it's not what you wanted to hear, don't react negatively, make assumptions, or immediately discount a sexual relationship with them. There are precautions that can be taken and ways around risk. Let them explain their situation, listen carefully, ask questions, and then do your own research. If you're really cool, you'll make self-deprecating jokes to put your partner at ease. ("You're worried about *me* rejecting *you*? What about when I get attached and you dump me in six months?") This kind

→

of reaction breeds more honesty in the dating world, which will mean more responsible sexual behavior, which will mean less STD transmission. Woohoo!

❷ The natural, knee-jerk inclination to dump someone when they admit, *after* you've already slept with them, to having an STD. You'll understandably think, "What an asshole! How could my partner do this? To betray my trust and risk my health like that—inexcusable!" We wouldn't be surprised if you never spoke to this person again, and neither should they.

But sometimes getting royally fucked over makes the heart grow fonder (see **rose-colored hindsight**). That's life's sick sense of humor. We sometimes fall in love, or stay in love, with those who don't deserve us. If you don't count the lying, the irresponsible behavior, the complete lack of respect for you, and the self-delusion, your partner's probably a great catch! You need to decide whether you're willing to give them the benefit of the doubt.

People make mistakes and they conceal STDs—out of denial, ignorance, or a series of rationalizations: "Risk of transmission is so low, why mention it?" Or "I don't want to lose *another* partner over this." Or "Everyone else is lying about this shit; why should I tell the truth?" Or "We're using barrier protection, so I don't need to mention it." Or "If they don't ask, I'm not gonna tell." Or "I look and feel healthy, so I must be!" Of course, there's a difference between not telling someone you have herpes or H.P.V. (which can be treated but have no cure) and not telling someone you had a bout of chlamydia ten years ago that was cleared up with antibiotics.

Whether you give someone a second chance depends on the circumstances and where you draw the line. And giving them a second chance doesn't mean letting them off them hook. Let your partner know the terms under which they can earn your trust again. If you decide to kick them to the curb and let them rot there,

S

allow yourself to mourn the end of the relationship and then follow our 10 steps for mending a broken heart (see page 7).

Either way, you need to find out as much good information as possible about the infection your partner has/had. PlannedParenthood.org, AshaSTD.org, and your own doctor are all good places to start. And from now on, be sure to have that awkward and painful discussion about sexual history with any potential partners *before* you get naked. Because, as anyone who's had this kind of STD scare knows, it can be much more awkward and painful after the fact.

stealth dump

When you don't **pad the fall** first.

sympathy fuck

❶ **Rebound sex** achieved primarily by milking your genuine post-breakup heartbreak for all it's worth in front of an understanding, attractive, and perhaps naïve soul: "I'm just *sooooo* lonely [*sniffle*], I just need someone to hold me in their arms to reassure me that the world is still a kind, warm place [*sigh*]. . . ." **Faux hawks** who don't have hearts to be broken to begin with just **fake it**. ❷ Sex with someone you are not particularly attracted to or don't necessarily want to do, but you do them anyway because you feel sorry for them because their heart was trampled (by you or someone else). A.k.a. charity work (most often used as a negative rebuttal, as in "I don't *do* charity work." Oh, *snap*!) See also **one for the road**, **second-chance sex**.

T

Talk, the

The big speech, prepared and delivered by the dumper, which definitively ends the relationship. Almost always preceded by the four words "**We need to talk**." The Talk invariably creates an awkward power dynamic, whereby the initiator immediately has all the hand, and with all that hand proceeds to figuratively face-slap, choke, and pull out the nose hairs of their audience-of-one until said audience is utterly humiliated, speechless, and fighting back tears—for more often than not, the Talk is not expected nor welcomed by its intended. However, if delivered adeptly, the Talk can be made as painless as possible. Avoid **clichés**, **big fat lies**, and the **cold hard truth**; do not give the Talk over a **last supper**, on a **chopping block** that's too public, or with malicious intent (see **posttraumatic stress dis**). Keep it

short, sweet, and sincere, and you will avoid getting literally slapped in the face.

tattoos

❶ Body art featuring your current partner's name or likeness on your arm, boob, lower back, ass, etc., as a symbol of your eternal love and commitment. Getting one (or matching ones) pretty much ensures that the tat will outlast the relationship. Perhaps the personality traits of people who choose to get such a tattoo in the first place—creativeness, unconventionality, spontaneity—are the same traits that make long-term commitment difficult for them. Hello, Dave Navarro and Carmen Electra? Their tattoos took more time to ink than their marriage took to fail. Personalized tattoos may also be a subconscious, last-ditch effort to save a relationship that the couple knows, deep down in their souls somewhere, is not working. Tats are the next best thing to marriage or handcuffs. Show everyone just how much you love your partner and you might start believing it, too. Tattoos may scream "CC 4eva." But, to paraphrase Shakespeare, wethinks the tattooed doth protest too much. And so, that heart with your lover's initials ends up looking like a cry for help. And once the relationship ends, it just looks stupid.

❷ A desperate measure by the recently dumped to prove their commitment and devotion to their ex. Forgive the recently brokenhearted, for they know not what they do.

❸ If your personality and personal style tend toward the alternative, a good way to **mark the occasion** of moving on from a bad breakup.

tear jerking

When a recent dumpee rents a super-sad movie for the cathartic release it provides—it's an excuse to totally lose your shit without feeling like a loser about it. Because sometimes it's a relief to weep over something that's guaranteed to be over in two hours, rather than the current heartache that feels like it's going to hurt for at least a decade. Popular titles include *Eternal Sunshine of the Spotless Mind, Secrets and Lies, Magnolia, Beaches, Once Were Warriors,* and *The Way We Were.*

Teflon breakup

A breakup that just won't stick, typically because the person you're trying to reject keeps rejecting your attempts to dump them. They either play **goalie** by arguing against your reasons for the breakup, or they condescendingly dismiss

→

your attempt as a silly little temper tantrum you'll get over in a day, or they figuratively close their ears and start singing, "La la la, I can't hear you" (on rare occasions they will do this literally). You may tell your partner that you think things are getting too serious and that it's probably best if you spent some time apart, but you'd still be up for "hanging out," which most people–even those with only a rudimentary knowledge of the language of love–know translates into "I'd like to sleep with other people, but would be happy to continue sleeping with you when it's convenient for me." Teflon-coated dumpees do not hear this. And so when they discover that you've reposted your **online dating** ad with the "Interested in 'play'" field checked off, they will call up their friends to get their advice, knowing full well that if they call you on it, you'll give them more bad news they don't want to hear. A.k.a. "Oh no you *di'nt*."

therapy fuck

The sexual equivalent of an hour on the couch with a really good shrink or an affirming life coach. Or at least that's the basic idea, even if the results aren't always quite what you intended. But then again, we know plenty of people whose therapists make them feel like shit, too. Unlike real therapy (or perhaps a Vicodin), sex is always free (and often easier to score than a Vicodin, too). The purpose of a therapy fuck is to take your mind off the gnawing heartache of a breakup, however briefly. It's not meant to be a permanent cure, but if you can forget, for an hour or two, that you're a pathetic, cuckolded loser who's still head-over-heels in love with an even bigger loser, then the therapy fuck has done its job. Caution: Side effects may include exaggerated feeling of well-being, depersonalization (unreal feeling), hallucinations, impaired concentration, memory loss, paranoia, sleepiness, rapid mood shifts, thoughts of harming yourself, hiccups, tooth

T

→

grinding, acne, agitation, constipation, anxiety, decreased sex drive, loose stool, difficulty with ejaculation, dizziness, dry mouth, nausea, fatigue, gas, speech problems, headache, decreased appetite, hair loss, grandiose thoughts and feelings, and generally inappropriate and out-of-control behavior. A.k.a. heartbreak sex. See also **rebound sex**.

thinking negatively

The third step of the **healing process**: referring to your ex exclusively as **Fuckface** and avoiding **rose-colored hindsight**. See also "How to Get Over a Breakup (in Ten Easy Steps)" (page 7).

thinking positively

The final step of the **healing process**, as celebrated by Gloria Gaynor in the 1978 anthem "**I Will Survive**." You might get **closure** (or you might just realize you don't need it, which is its own kind of closure), you'll finally **metabolize** your ex, and you'll realize that it's about time you treated yourself to a **sorbet/therapy fuck/online date**. In other words, you'll finally realize that it really *wasn't* you, it was them. See also **mourning period (for the dumpee)** and "How to Get Over a Breakup (in Ten Easy Steps)" (page 7).

trading up

Breaking up with someone for a newer/richer/smarter/younger/thinner/better-looking model. Common among social climbers, gold diggers, and insecure fucks.

T

U

ultima-dump

When a dumpee resorts to threats to avoid being broken up with: "I'll kill myself," "I'll post naked pics of you on my blog," "I'll stalk you," "I'll cry," etc. It's a desperate last move made by someone who's not smooth enough to pull off a **Teflon breakup** and who doesn't have the sense of self-preservation to just walk away after the **leg-clinging** fails. Giving in to an ultima-dump is like negotiating with terrorists, and we all know how well that works out these days. Instead, remove any sharp objects or incriminating photos from the immediate surrounding area, and block your ears as you walk away. If you think the death thing is more than an idle threat, then call 911 or your dumpee's best friend and put *them* on suicide watch. Then change your phone number. See also **bunny-boiler**.

unilateral dump

Breaking up in your heart and mind, and then behaving as if you're single *before* you've informed your partner of the breakup. You're acting alone, without consideration for any other parties involved, based on either faulty intelligence (e.g. a base and baseless rumor concerning your partner's extracurriculars) or your own lack of intelligence. So, at the beginning of a boys'/girls' weekend away, you decide "I'm done, that's it," and proceed to have your orifices poked by the hottie from the hotel bar, while your fiancé back home is calligraphically handwriting all 250 of your wedding invitations. A.k.a. chumpifying.

BEST MOVIE BR
OF ALL TIME: A

> "A relationship, I think, is like a shark, you know? It has to constantly move forward or it dies. And I think what we got on our hands is a dead shark."

V

Valentine's Day massacre

Dumping someone on V-Day. It's a photo finish as to which is worse: dumping them on the actual holiday, dumping them the day before so you don't have to get them a gift and they have to spend International Love Day curled up in the fetal position, or dumping them the day after so they can suffer the additional mortification of knowing that you sat there and ate those chocolate-covered strawberries that they'd slaved over all week, while rehearsing in your mind the breakup speech you planned to deliver in 24 hours' time (see also **last supper**). Obviously, the more distance you can place between V-Day and the breakup, the better—but then again, you don't want to drag things out if you're 100 percent sure. Oh god, don't make us pick! Can't you people just take a look at a calendar every once in a while? See also **crappy holidays**.

wakaresase

A Japanese cottage industry that translates roughly as "business to force breakup of a couple." Wakaresase companies are a hybrid of private detective agencies, brothels, and the Secret Service: their staff of attractive young women and men will seduce, date, dump, and disappear on someone for a (hefty) paycheck. Maybe you want to break up your wife's affair with her tennis coach, so you hire a stud to lure her away, and right when she's forgotten all about how much work her backhand needed, the secret agent goes **A.W.O.L.** and she's once again a "faithful" wife. Or perhaps you want to divorce your husband but can't think of a legitimate reason, so you pay a company like Ladies Secret Service or the Japan Research Institute on Male-Female Issues to ensnare the guy in a one-night stand with a "flight attendant" . . . which just happens to be caught on videotape. Of course, this is in a country that sells schoolgirls' used undies out of vending machines. Stateside, things are a little more tame and lighthearted— see **Dear John dot coms** for the kind of sanitized breakup professionals at your service in the U.S.

we need to talk

The four little words that sound the death knell of your relationship. See **Talk, the**.

white lies

The little fictions that make breakups bearable. Breakup white lies are mostly lies of omission; for example, "I'm not ready for a relationship right now" generally means "I'm not *ever* going to be ready for a relationship with *you*" (see **clichés** and the **fortune cookie rule**). We withhold the **cold hard truth** from each other because dumpees are frail little creatures, and there are only so many "facts" they can handle at a time like this. They don't need to know about the overwhelming sense of relief that washed over you once you decided to end the relationship—what they need to hear is that the decision was "hard, so very hard." They don't need to know that it will take you approximately five minutes to get over this dump, and they certainly don't need to know that you've been ogling the manager at the local indie bookstore for about three months (*especially* if you haven't acted on that ogling—see **someone else**). It's okay to

act sadder than you feel, and it's okay to tell them, "Yes, if I ever change my mind, I'll let you know" (see **noncommittal breakup**). Finally, if your dumpee tries to lure you into **one for the road** and you'd honestly rather floss with Mike Wallace's pubic hair than get naked with them tonight, then it's perfectly acceptable to tell them, "I just don't think that's right for me to do to you. You don't know how tempted I am, but I know that the best thing to do is to walk away right now." If you can't tell the difference between little white lies and an **overcompensation** or a noncommittal breakup, then ask yourself this: *Am I telling the fib to make this breakup easier for me, or for my dumpee?* If it's the latter, it's a white lie, and we've got your back. If it's the former, then you need to go all the way back to "A" and reread this book one more time, our friend. A.k.a. truthiness.

white-out

The act of breaking up with someone by suddenly avoiding all eye contact—you simply look away every time they come near you until they get the point. This is particularly common at the end of a casual relationship between coworkers or between two people who move in the same loose social circle, i.e. when going **A.W.O.L.** simply isn't an option, much to your irritation. You'll need eyeballs of steel to pull this off, and even then, there's no guarantee that your dumpee won't force an embarrassingly noisy show-down at the water cooler. And if they don't and you "get away with it"? Must be nice, having no moral compass.

win-win breakup

A passive-aggressive yet genius breakup strategy whereby you come out on top no matter what happens. Let's say you're feeling a little lukewarm about your relationship: You could break up with your partner, but you're too lazy to do the heavy emotional lifting it requires. So instead, you suggest a three-way with your partner and their hottie roommate. Either your partner dumps you when you refuse to drop the subject, or you get that three-way—win-win!

W.M.D.s

The exaggerations or fibs that a dumpee tries to pass off as truth in order to convince their dumper that they're so over the relationship, including but not limited to: ❶ "I'm so glad we decided to end our relation-ship." (A.k.a. the retroactive **mutual decision**.) ❷ "I'm so in love with my new partner,

→

it makes me realize that I'd never really been in love before." ❸ "I'm so busy right now, I don't know how I ever found time to date!" ❹ "So it turns out that I *can* orgasm during intercourse after all!"

If you dumped this person and then they call you to tell you all that, their new partner/orgasm/overall feeling of well-being is as likely to exist as Saddam's *nucular* stash.

worst-case scenario breakup

A breakup that is precipitated by your own personal Watergate move: you suspect that your partner might be cheating on you/stealing your stuff/selling naked photos of you online, so you break into their e-mail account/follow them home from work/read their text messages while they take a shower . . . and discover that all your worst fears are true. In other words, you weren't suffering from

Chicken Little syndrome after all—you just happen to have a good nose for lying dogs.

First, the obligatory slap on the wrist for invading your partner's privacy—shame on you! Everyone has a right to privacy, even the two-timing, scum-sucking **bottom-feeders** who weren't loved enough by their mamas. Speaking of mamas, didn't yours tell you two wrongs don't make a right?

Second, do not attempt to use this unethically discovered information to "accidentally" bump into your partner during a secret rendezvous. Those kinds of scenes always play better on daytime soaps. Rather, immediately and humbly confess your crime—this will serve the dual purpose of providing a segue into your accusation while pre-empting any beef they could have with you. For dramatic effect, try, "I did a terrible thing for which I'm truly sorry, and I don't expect you to forgive me for it. [*suspenseful pause*] But you did something far, far worse." Or perhaps, "What have you got to say for

→

yourself, Pigfucker?" (Hey, some people like to start out on the offensive when they know they've lost a bit of the moral high ground.) You did something wrong, but you can't undo that now; you can only apologize for it. Besides, what else are you going to do? Act like you didn't find out all that stuff and then continue sleeping with someone who may well be shtupping the entire clientele at your local Fluff 'n' Fold? Hire a P.I. to tail them and get real evidence? (They're only glorified snoopers like you, and your snoopin' don't cost a thang.) Don't feel like you owe your partner forgiveness just because you snooped. Like all good lawyers would tell you, that's another trial for another day, and that evidence is not to be entered into this hearing.

Once you deliver your scum-of-the-earth speech in all its daytime-soap glory, your partner will have the chance to defend themselves (as if there's just cause), get pissed at you for breaking in to their e-mail (a petty crime, at least compared to their felony), and/or try to win you back (not that you'd take them). But more importantly, their retort will help you decide if there's even the slightest chance this piece of garbage might be worth recycling. If not, it'll give you some closure. At the very least, you'll get to watch them squirm.

If, on the other hand, you have "accidentally" found a way to break in to your chief suspect's secret life but have yet to exploit it, here's the right thing to do, and our official policy on the matter: Don't dig. A mature relationship is built on trust and communication; if you suspect that trust has been violated, then you communicate your fears like a grownup. Amateur detective work is nothing but another violation of trust, made even worse if you discover they've done absolutely nothing wrong. Consider worst-case scenario breakups an exception to the rule—the rare instance doesn't justify *you* snooping on your partner any more than your chain-smoking grandmother who lived until the grand old age of ninety-nine justifies your nicotine habit. Chances are, you're simply suffering from a nasty case of Chicken Little syndrome.

But what if you're convinced to the core of your being that it's more than that? And what if there's good circumstantial evidence (e.g. they recently posted an **online dating** ad and you're supposed to be "exclusive") *and* you've known them to lie in the past when confronted? (For the record, a spat with your partner over their crush on Lindsay Lohan is not considered grounds for suspicion.)

Honestly? *We* would dig. Hey, people lie and cheat all the time. It's not right, but them's the facts of life. If *you* were inundated with e-mails asking how to get away with cheating, like we are, you'd lose a little faith in humanity, too. And when you find out that someone you've been dating isn't who you thought they were in one regard (e.g. they log on to dating sites after you've fallen asleep at night),

then it's hard to trust them in another respect. They become an unreliable source of information to you, so you seek a second, secret opinion.

Oh sure, go ahead and tell us that this only creates a downward spiral of mistrust. Whine to us that even if we discover nothing's amiss, something's already been spoiled. Sic the A.C.L.U. on us. But things were spoiled long before we got here—by all the cheaters of the world who have created an environment of suspicion. If they can't stand the heat (or lack thereof) of monogamy, why do they insist on getting into—and staying in—monogamous relationships under false pretenses? They've got to get out of the relationship or into an open one. "But it's more complicated than that!" the philanderers cry. There's always an excuse. And so rationalization begets cheating, which begets lying, which begets suspicion, which begets digging. It's a vicious cycle, but hey, the cheaters started it. And suspicious minds with faithful hearts are higher up on the

→

evolutionary ladder than philanderers. We'll take the faithful's side every time.

Do as we say or do as we do, it's your call. And if you *are* wrong? Prepare to eat some serious humble pie at the upcoming family gathering (more badminton, anyone?). And don't expect your partner to eat your pie for a least a month. A.k.a. snoop dog, the two-wrongs rule.

Do you really have to attend your friend's poetry slam if there's a chance you might run into the asshole who just broke your heart? Is it bad manners to bring a hot date to your weekly Pictionary gathering if your heartbroken ex is on the other team? Just ask the chart: Locate your Defense Readiness Condition, or DEFCON level (thanks, U.S. military!), on one axis and the occasion in question on the opposite axis. Your prescription is found at the point where these two meet. Who said math is hard?

Wedding

Concert or Reading

Friend's Birthday Party

House Party

Intimate Dinner Party

DEFCON 1
(loss of appetite, self-destructive behavior, idle thoughts of suicide)

DEFCON 2
(bitter, angry, contemplating revenge)

This is the only excuse for missing a friend or family member's wedding. Take comfort in small mercies.

Suck it up and show up. Consider skipping the open bar to avoid making a scene.

Stay home and write your own bad angst-ridden love songs or poetry.

If it's a close friend's gig, dress to the nines and bring a hot date. If not, stay home and surf online personals.

Stay home. The birthday boy or girl will understand. Buy your own cake and ice cream. Eat it all yourself.

Arrange to take the birthday boy or girl out for dinner/drinks another night. Then sleep with said birthday boy/girl.

Stay home, get a bottle of seven-dollar merlot, and Netflix *House Party*.

Stay away. The cops will probably show up . . . not because of complaints about noise, but because you either tried to slap or suck face with your ex after one too many scotches on the rocks.

Stay home, order takeout for one, and rent any movie with a flower in its title as an excuse to shamelessly plow through an entire box of Kleenex: *Steel Magnolias, White Oleander, Magnolia, The Rose, Bed of Roses, Driving Miss Daisy*. See also **tear jerking**.

Stay home, because if you go, instead of blurting out "Baby fish mouth" during a round of Pictionary, you might scream "I hope you die alone and miserable!"

→

	DEFCON 3 (you don't want them back, but you don't want them to meet anyone else yet)
Wedding	Ask the wedding planner ahead of time to seat you at the table with the other hot singles, and to seat your ex at Aunt Edna's table.
Concert or Reading	Show up, be polite, and leave as soon as it's over, as if you have somewhere exciting to be.
Friend's Birthday Party	Show up and practice being normal.
House Party	Stay away, because you *will* witness your ex talking to new and interesting people while you'll feel stranded and abandoned over by the bean dip.
Intimate Dinner Party	Stay home—you're too likely to hear something you don't want to know. Instead, talk to a really good friend who will blow smoke up your ass.

DEFCON 4
(it's for the best, but it's still mildly awkward)

DEFCON 5
(free at last, free at last!)

Have a drink, do the chicken dance, try to be happy someone else's relationship worked out.

Do not nosedive for the bouquet or garter. To do so will scream to your ex, "It's not that I didn't want to get married, I just didn't want to marry *you*." And that's harsh.

Go—at least you'll have something (your mutual friend's gig) to make small talk about with your ex.

Show up unless the band or book sucks.

Show up—you'll give everyone something to gossip about.

Stop short of jumping out of the birthday cake.

Stop by on your way to a fabulously exciting dinner party across town.

Go, but do not be the first person to karaoke, the first person to dance on furniture, or the first person to make out with a stranger in the middle of the crowded room.

Show up, but make sure you're not on the same Pictionary team.

Show up, but don't bring a date, especially if that date is younger/hotter/richer/funnier than your ex. In fact, be the bigger person, send your regrets to the host, and then enjoy a date with that younger/hotter/richer/funnier person in the privacy of your own home.

Dumping Ditties: The Top 100 Breakup Songs of All Time

1. "50 Ways to Leave Your Lover" – **PAUL SIMON**

2. "Absolutely Zero" – **JASON MRAZ**

3. "Against All Odds" – **PHIL COLLINS (OR THE POSTAL SERVICE VERSION)**

4. "All Alone Am I" – **BRENDA LEE**

5. "All By Myself" – **ERIC CARMEN (DEFINITELY NOT THE CELINE DION VERSION)**

6. "All My Ex's Live in Texas" – **GEORGE STRAIT**

7. "Alone Again (Naturally)" – **GILBERT O'SULLIVAN**

8. "Another Lonely Day" – **BEN HARPER**

9. "Apart" – **THE CURE**

10. "Are You Lonesome Tonight?" – **ELVIS PRESLEY**

11. "Ballad of Big Nothing" – **ELLIOTT SMITH**

12. "Black" – **PEARL JAM**

13. "Blackout" – **MUSE**

14. "Blue Moon Revisited" – **COWBOY JUNKIES**

15. "Can't Stand Losing You" – **THE POLICE**

16. "Careless Whisper" – **WHAM!**

17. "Crazy" – **PATSY CLINE OR WILLIE NELSON**

36 "Hopelessly Devoted to You" – **OLIVIA NEWTON-JOHN (FROM THE *GREASE* SOUNDTRACK)**

37 "How Can You Be Sure?" – **RADIOHEAD**

38 "I Fall to Pieces" – **PATSY CLINE**

39 "I Hope You're Happy Now" – **ELVIS COSTELLO**

40 "I Never Cared for You" – **WILLIE NELSON**

41 "I Used to Love Her" – **GUNS N' ROSES**

42 "I Want You" – **ELVIS COSTELLO**

43 "I Will Survive" – **GLORIA GAYNOR**

44 "If I Can't Have You" – **YVONNE ELLIMAN**

45 "I'm So Lonesome I Could Cry" – **TAKE YOUR PICK: HANK WILLIAMS, ELVIS PRESLEY, COWBOY JUNKIES, OR JOHNNY CASH**

46 "I'm Sorry" – **BRENDA LEE**

47 "It's a Heartache" – **JUICE NEWTON OR BONNIE TYLER**

48 "It's Not Right, But It's Okay" – **WHITNEY HOUSTON (THE THUNDERPUSS REMIX)**

49 "It's Over" – **ROY ORBISON**

50 "I've Been Loving You Too Long" – **OTIS REDDING**

51 "Killing Me Softly with His Song" – **FUGEES OR ROBERTA FLACK**

52 "Last Goodbye" – **JEFF BUCKLEY**

70 "Separate Ways" – **JOURNEY**

71 "She Is Gone" – **WILLIE NELSON**

72 "She's Got You" – **PATSY CLINE**

73 "Should've Been in Love" – **WILCO**

74 "Since I Don't Have You" – **GUNS N' ROSES**

75 "Since U Been Gone" – **KELLY CLARKSON**

76 "So Lonely" – **THE POLICE**

77 "So Wrong" – **PATSY CLINE**

78 "Soma" – **SMASHING PUMPKINS**

79 "Somebody That I Used to Know" – **ELLIOTT SMITH**

80 "Strange" – **PATSY CLINE**

81 "Sweet Dreams" – **PATSY CLINE**

82 "Tainted Love" – **SOFT CELL**

83 "The Seventh Stranger" – **DURAN DURAN**

84 "The Sign" – **ACE OF BASE**

85 "There's a Tear in My Beer" – **HANK WILLIAMS**

86 "These Arms of Mine" – **OTIS REDDING**

87 "This Woman's Work" – **KATE BUSH**

88 "Total Eclipse of the Heart" – **BONNIE TYLER**